Also by G

Flatiron

The Content of Their Character

Phutile to Phinally

10,000 Losses and One Life as a Phillies Fan

Gerard Shields

HILLIARD HARRIS

P.O. Box 275
Boonsboro, Maryland 21713-0275

Non-Fiction
The opinions expressed here are those of the author and not necessarily
those of Hilliard & Harris.

Phutile to Phinally Copyright © 2009 By Gerard Shields

Fenton Press
First Edition-December 2008
ISBN 1-59133-291-5
978-1-59133-291-6

Book Design: S. A. Reilly
Cover Illustration © S. A. Reilly
Manufactured/Printed in the United States of America
2009

To Mr. George Post, the greatest Phillies fan I ever knew."

Acknowledgements

A shout out to the ladies, Stephanie and Shawn Reilly, for their unwavering support and for believing in me and making dreams come true.

A hearty yo out to Martin "The Duke" DeAngelis, who gave the manuscript a read and made some helpful suggestions. And lastly, a big thank you to Sean Lengell of The Washington Times, whose enthusiasm provided the gasoline to keep this book motoring.

And with deepest gratitude to my father, Fred, for making me a Phillies fan.

Prologue

I never chose to be a Philadelphia Phillies baseball fan. I was born into it.

My father, Fred Shields, was like most Philadelphians, an avid Phillies fan for as long as he could remember. Starting in the 1930s, dad seemed to follow every Phillies game, pitch by pitch. And after he returned from World War II and married mom, he even taught her how to keep the score of games when he had to work nights.

Like a teacher grading a student's paper, dad would comb over mom's score sheet the next morning. It allowed him to follow the previous night's game batter by batter. She learned how to scrawl 1B to signal a single or a K for a strikeout and the ultimate—HR for a home run.

He worked as a bus mechanic for the city transportation system, which earned him a free pass to ride wherever he wanted to in the city. He used it for two occasions: to get to work and to travel to Phillies games.

He would take the Route 22 bus, which rolled along Lehigh Avenue to 22nd Street and our city's monolith to baseball, Connie Mack Stadium, originally called Shibe Park. And when I was old enough, a little taller than the knees on dad's 6-feet-3 frame, he would take me with him.

Most trips ended in futility, a Phillies loss. The Philadelphia Phillies have lost more games—over 10,000—than any other team in American sports history.

Sure Boston and Chicago fans had to endure their World Series droughts. Both the Atlanta Braves, who once played in Boston, and the

Chicago Cubs were in the league seven years longer than the Phillies. But those teams were comfortably behind the Phillies in the loss columns by 319 and 575 games respectively.

Philadelphia fans were subjected to what could be likened to a baseball version of the Chinese water torture, a slow drip of losses that wounded every Phillies baseball fan when they picked up the morning sports section or turned on the local news. It didn't help that we were two hours south on the interstate of the dreaded New York Yankees, who have won 26 baseball world championships.

In a 1978 interview with The New York Times, famous Philadelphia area author, James Michener, may have summed up what being a Phillies fan really felt like.

"Since 1915, I have been cheering for the Philadelphia Phillies and if that doesn't take character, what does?" Michener said. "In such circumstances it is traditional to say 'I supported them in good years and bad.' There were no good years, I cheered in bad and worse."

Why should a city be so affected by the performance of a baseball team? It was a matter of pride. Going back to when the Greeks first held their Olympics, city pride rose and fell on the performance of the athletes who represented them. And since baseball was America's pastime, Phillies fans saw their team as a representation of their city and thus themselves to the rest of the nation. As goes the Phillies, so goes Philadelphia. We are a tribe, they are our warriors.

"A baseball club is part of the chemistry of a city," New York Yankees President Michael Burke told a 1971 New York City Council Committee. "A game just isn't an athletic contest. It's a picnic, a kind of town meeting."

In Philadelphia, expectations were low. Their first season in 1883 was their worst, with the team winning only 17 of 89 games. The oldest one-name, one-city franchise in baseball, the Phillies lost 100 games 13 times, a league record, and finished in last place 31 times in their 125 years.

Phillies managers held their job an average of 2 ½ years, with only 12 of them lasting four years or more. Between 1917 and 1943, the club had one winning season, dropping 100 games a year during a 14-year span beginning in 1938.

"Examining the franchise's history is akin to reading the Book of Job," Philadelphia Inquirer sports reporter Frank Fitzpatrick wrote in his 2001 Phillies diatribe *You Can't Lose Them All*. "The Philadelphia Phillies were expected to lose just as the New York Yankees were expected to win."

Phillies stalwarts, however, say the futility of the team is exaggerated. No one mentions that during their span they won 9,000 games. And that the Phillies were one of the oldest teams around adds to the potential for losses. The team has only had one 100-loss season in the last 62 years and over the past four decades have been one of the more successful franchises.

I was born in 1961 and it would be several years before I would consciously join the Phillies faithful as a consenting fan. But by the time I was 8-years-old and able to join dad at the games, everyone was still talking about the slide.

It happened in 1964. The Phillies had a 6 ½ game lead over the St. Louis Cardinals and the Cincinnati Reds with 12 games left in the season. Most observers figured the Phils a cinch to win the pennant just by pulling a baseball version of the rope-a-dope, make no mistakes and victory was ours. The team even had the World Series tickets already printed.

They had routinely beaten teams with future Hall of Famers on them, guys like Willie Mays, Bob Gibson, Sandy Koufax and Hank Aaron.

"The '64 Phillies were a team that overachieved for most of the year, a team that left its heart on the field, a team that strengthened our love and appreciation for baseball," wrote Philadelphia Inquirer sportswriter Sam Carchidi.

But it wasn't meant to be.

The Phillies went on to lose 10 straight games while the Cardinals went 9-1 to capture the flag marking the greatest late-season collapse in baseball history. It became known as "The Phold of '64."

The Phils weren't even supposed to be in the hunt, predicted to finish somewhere in the middle of the pack. But its mastermind coach, Gene Mauch, used a system of switching and resting players and managed to coax 90 wins out of the first 150 games.

Their hot young star, and their first black superstar, Richie Allen, hit .318 with 29 homers many of them out of the park. Their veteran right fielder, Johnny Callison, added 31 homers and knocked in 104 runs.

Philadelphia was in a frenzy as the team closed in on their first pennant in 14 years.

In addition, they had two pitchers flirting with 20-game seasons. Future Hall of Famer Jim Bunning went 19-8 while lefty Chris Short amassed a 17-9 record. The jewel of the season came on Father's Day when Bunning pitched a perfect game, something my father remembered til the day he died.

Some would say the slide began when Cincinnati's Chico Ruiz stole home in the sixth inning on Sept. 21 to give the Reds a 1-0 victory. Mauch, who earned the nickname "The Little General" for his explosive manner, would be blamed for the team's collapse.

Over 40 years later, many say he panicked, choosing to pitch his two tired aces for the remainder of the season. In that stretch, Bunning lost three games. But the Phillies had other problems. It's big hitting first baseman Frank Thomas, who had been acquired from the New York Mets and hit seven home runs, broke his thumb just as the cave in began.

"You were like a zombie," Phillies fan and New Jersey financial analyst Lloyd Adams would tell The New York Times during the commemoration of the team's 10,000 loss in 2007. "There was nothing to live for. The whole city was in mourning. A year in Vietnam was not as bad as those two weeks."

The Cardinals went on to beat the New York Yankees in the World Series while Philadelphia's reputation as The City of Losers when it came to baseball was being cemented. It would be more than a decade before the Phillies would get their shot to avenge the '64 fold.

"It's easy to see why generations of Philadelphians never followed the examples of Chicago or Boston fans in believing their team was cursed," Fitzpatrick wrote. "Cursed would have been an improvement."

Chapter 1
The Whiz Kids

As I sprouted as a Phillies fan, dad was still talking about The Whiz Kids. The 1950 Phillies won the National League pennant for only the second time in team history, the first occurring 35 years earlier in 1915.

"Bicentennials come once every 200 years," famous sports writer Red Smith once wrote. "Pennants come more often in Betsy Ross's town, but not much."

They were dubbed The Whiz Kids because of their youth with the average player being 26. They were picked to finish 4th but gained stellar performances from players such as relief pitcher Jim Konstanty, who won 16 games and recorded 22 saves to become the first relief pitcher in history to ever be named the league's Most Valuable Player.

Konstanty threw what he called a "palmball" that froze batters. At one point in the season he pitched 22 innings without allowing a run.

"Jim had a burning desire to be the best," Eddie Sawyer, manager of the team, once said of his ace.

Unlike the Phillies tradition of having owners unwilling to spend money on the team, Robert Carpenter spent $2 million just in bonuses for his young players. The Phils even donned new red and white pin-striped uniforms, signaling what they hoped would be a new era of winning.

Starting pitcher Robin Roberts was the team workhorse. With a slicing curve and laser beam control that paralyzed hitters, Roberts accumulated seven straight victories, including three consecutive shutouts on his way to winning 20 games.

Phillies fans were gleeful. On Sept. 3, an estimated 30,000 Phillies faithful met the team at the 30th Street train station after the Phillies 14-game road trip where they had won 11.

Even sportswriters covering the team wore Phillies hats and shirts in the press box.

Though it seemed that the Phillies would glide to their first pennant in 35 years, Sawyer cautioned his young group that the season wasn't over. He was right. The Phillies lost seven of their last nine, while their rival Brooklyn Dodgers captured 12 of their last 15 games to pull within two wins of the Phillies.

On the final weekend of the season, the two teams played each other with Dodgers needing two wins to force a pennant playoff. The Dodgers won the first game, 7-3, meaning that if they won the final game, the two teams would be tied for first. Such a result was one that the staggering Phillies wanted to avoid.

In their final game of the season on a mild sunny afternoon, the Phillies scored the first run of the game in the sixth inning only to have the Dodgers tie it in their turn at bat.

In the ninth inning, center fielder Richie Ashburn was playing shallow and picked up a hit on a short hop, throwing it to home plate and nailing what would have been the Dodgers winning run. In what is called the greatest throw in Phillies history, Ashburn's pitch beat the runner by 20-feet.

In the top of the tenth inning, Phillie Dick Sisler hit a three-run homer to win the pennant. Fans spilled into the street blaring horns, blowing whistles and tossing firecrackers as a mob welcomed the team home at the train station.

In talking about The Whiz Kids, dad would focus on the man he believed to be the greatest center fielder of all time: Ashburn. The Nebraska native had a .311 career batting average with the Phils, having come up through the franchise's farm system.

He spent 12 years with the Phillies as their leadoff hitter, base stealer and patrol man of the outfield, known for shagging fly balls unreachable by other players. Dad would tell me that

Ashburn had a unique gift. As soon as he heard the crack of the bat, he knew where the ball would land and would turn and run to that spot.

He won two National League batting titles and led the league in hits three times. He still holds the major league record for most years—four—with 500 or more fly ball catches. He was rookie of the year in 1948 and hit at least .300 with the Phillies eight times, still holding the Phillies record for playing in consecutive games with 730.

"He runs like he has twin motors in his pants," baseball great Ted Williams once said of Ashburn.

Dad wasn't alone in his belief of Ashburn's greatness. In his 1990 classic baseball book, "Men At Work," writer George Will argued that Ashburn posted the same numbers and rivaled the greatest center fielders of the time, such as Mays and Mickey Mantle.

"Well positioned and intelligently anticipating," Will wrote of Ashburn.

Despite his success, Ashburn—who had frequent confrontations with the press, was denied entrance to the baseball Hall of Fame by the sports writers for 33 years.

"If he had put up most of those numbers in New York City, under the media microscope, he would already be enshrined in Cooperstown," Will wrote.

Despite winning the National League pennant, the Phillies lost in four games to the dreaded Yankees, losing three of the games by one run and denying its yearning city its first baseball world championship.

For the remainder of the decade the Phillies would toggle between fourth and fifth place, never regaining their championship form. The year after their World Series appearance, they tumbled to fifth place, an event that was blamed on swelled heads.

The only players repeating their strong previous season were Roberts, Sisler and Ashburn. Ashburn once again led the league in hits and catches while finishing second in stolen bases. He finished the season battling for the league batting title with a .344 average.

Sawyer tried to shock the team into action by banning luxuries during Spring Training in 1952. No wives, autos, swimming or golf were permitted, a move that backfired by alienating the ballplayers. The Phils finished fourth, costing Sawyer his job.

In addition to Ashburn, Roberts was having a Hall of Fame career. He had six consecutive 20 game seasons and won pitcher of the year honors twice and a player of the year award. Roberts had won more games than any Phillies pitcher since Grover Cleveland Alexander.

The year 1954 was memorable in Philadelphia baseball history because the Athletics left for Kansas City, leaving the Phillies sole control the city baseball diamond. A year later, Ashburn won his first batting title over Mays.

In 1957, the Phillies had another first when it hired shortstop Chico Fernandez as its first black player. The Phillies were the last team in the National League to integrate and in 1942 passed over Dodger great Roy Campenella, a three-time league MVP, because he was black.

Owner Bob Carpenter bore no shame over the dubious distinction.

"I'm not opposed to Negro players," Carpenter told the media. "But I'm not going to hire a player of any color or nationality just to have him on the team."

As the decade closed out, the Phillies once again sunk to the bottom the league finishing eighth. The only bright spot was Ashburn, who won another batting title and caught more fly balls than any other player.

Ashburn had 2,217 hits, more than any other Phillie until Mike Schmidt. Ashburn had a career average of .308.

Likewise, Phillies slugger Del Ennis consistently produced big hits, hitting 259 home runs with the Phillies and knocking in 1,124 runners, both club records until Schmidt arrived.

The decade that began with such hope and pride smoldered like embers as the era of the Whiz Kids evaporated. The Phillies finished in last place in 1959, the second consecutive year. Roberts lost more games than he won going 15-17 and even Ashburn's average dropped to .266. He was traded the

4

next winter to the new franchise, the New York Mets and the Phillies would once again face another decade of futility.

Chapter 2
My First Season

In the summer I was born, 1961, the Philadelphia Phillies lost 107 games, winning only 45, their eighth worst season ever.

The year was remembered most for a 23-game losing streak that got the club the nickname "The Team From Hell." But in true Philly form, several hundred fans were at the airport to greet the team when they returned home after the losing streak.

The players, however, didn't know what to expect. When the plane arrived, pitcher Frank Sullivan warned his teammates.

"Get off in twos and threes so they can't get us all with one burst. They're selling rocks at a dollar a pail."

Baseball player and comic Bob Uecker said he was once picked up and fined by the Philadelphia police for being drunk.

"Five hundred dollars for being drunk and $100 for being with the Phillies," Uecker said.

The Phillies finished an astonishing 46 games out of first place.

Under their fiery coach, Mauch, the Phils improved in 1962 to 81-80, their first winning record in seven years and an improvement of 34 games. In 1963, the club did better still, winning 87 games for a fourth-place finish. Their best ball was played during the last two months of the season, prompting the pennant-winning Dodgers to call the Phillies the best team in the National League.

"Awe, we just ought to let the Philllies go," Dodgers

General Manager Buzzy Bavasi suggested to the press of the World Series. "They played the best ball in the league the last two months."

Mauch would be most remembered, though, for dropping the pennant in '64.

"It was like watching somebody drown," Mauch told reporters.

When asked what he remembered most about the season, Mauch replied: "Every fucking pitch."

The major bright spot of the skid was the emergence of the first baseman, Allen. He earned his place on the team by his performance in the Phillies minor league club in Little Rock, Ark. Allen led the International League in triples, home runs and RBIs. He was brought up by the Phillies for the last seven games of 1963 and batted .292.

Allen was bitter toward the Phillies for sending him to Little Rock, known for its racism. But in 1964, Allen won the National League rookie of the year award, hitting .319 with 29 home runs, 91 runs batted in and a league-leading 125 runs.

Phillies historian Rich Westcott provided the best description of Allen: a racehorse body, rippled muscles and wrists like coiled springs.

Allen, however, also committed 40 errors and 138 strikeouts, earning him jeers from rabid Phillies fans. He didn't respond to criticism well.

In 1965, a year the Phillies would win 85 games and finish 11 ½ games out of first place, a string of Allen antics began. It started when he got into a fight with the team's white power-hitter, Thomas.

Thomas taunted Allen reportedly saying: "You're getting just like Cassius Clay—Muhammad Clay—always running off at the mouth."

"That don't go with me," Allen said before punching Thomas in the chest.

Thomas swung the bat he had in his hand and struck Allen on the left shoulder. Both powerful and much Thomas' junior, Allen lunged at the veteran as teammates pulled them apart. For his role in the fight, Thomas was released after the game, in

7

which he hit the game-winning home run. Some Phillies fans blamed the Thomas loss on Allen, who was often booed thereafter.

Allen started to become tardy for games and even missed a team train to New York.

While the team was floundering in the majors, it was revamping its minor league farm system by elevating Paul Owens to take over. Owens immediately fired eight scouts, some of them friends, and put two on probation. He himself had been a Phillies scout reaching back to 1955.

In 1966, the Phillies continued a long team tradition of making horrendous trades. They let go of a young pitcher named Ferguson Jenkins, trading him to Chicago because he was said to have a "suspect fastball."

Mauch likened trading Jenkins to getting rid of "a bag of garbage." Jenkins would go on to a Hall of Fame career, with many of his wins coming on the backs of the Phillies.

Allen had his biggest season ever in 1966 with 40 home runs and 110 runs batted in while hitting .317. Yet he continued to be a problem child on the team. In 1967, a year the Phillies finished fourth with 87 wins, Allen cut his hand in a strange incident.

He was pushing a car, he said, when he slipped, punching his right hand through a headlight. He severed two tendons and a nerve, almost crippling him.

Allen became an increasing distraction to the team. He fought management over money, repeatedly asked to be traded, sometimes failed to show up for games and in some cases, arrived drunk.

In 1968, the Phillies fired Gene Mauch, who still holds the distinction of being the Phillies manager with the most wins at 646 and most losses at 684. Many believed Allen's antics cost Mauch his job. The first baseman had missed two days of Spring Training without permission, showed up late for a New York game and injured himself horseback riding.

The Allen problems stretched into 1969 when he began scrawling phrases in the dirt near first base and moved his locker room into a storage area. He missed several team flights and games or arrived late.

When manager George Myatt took over the team from Mauch midway through the year, the first question from the press was obvious: how was he going to handle Allen?

"I don't think God Almighty himself could handle Richie Allen so all I can do is try," Myatt said

Chapter 3
The Greatest Player Ever

Maybe the way he blessed himself before batting caught my eye.

Or maybe I admired how he threw his body fearlessly at every skittering ground ball. He batted a mere .261, reaching base about once every four times at bat in his career. Yet to this day, Antonio Nemesio "Tony" Taylor remains my favorite Phillie of all time.

So that's why on my eighth birthday, I asked dad for the flannel Phillies uniform with the red script emblazoned across the front. The conflict began when the store clerk asked which number should be stitched on the back of the uniform. Before he could finish, I blurted out.

"No. 8! No. 8! Tony Taylor! No. 8!"

My enthusiasm embarrassed dad, who bowed his head for one reason: Tony Taylor was black. He's actually Afro-Cuban. He and his family fled their homeland before Fidel Castro's 1959 revolution.

The white store clerk looked up to see if dad would crack under his little boy's pressure.

"I thought you wanted No. 6," dad said, referring to Callison, the team's white right field hero.

"No, dad," I said. "You know Tony Taylor is my favorite."

"Are you sure?" dad asked, hoping persistence might wear me down. "Why don't you get No. 6? What's the difference?"

"No dad, it's got to be No. 8."

Dad worried about me walking around our all-white East Philadelphia neighborhood wearing the number of a black ballplayer. Yet I proudly wore that uniform through the neighborhood that day, even wearing it to my official Little League game for the Port Richmond Robins that night, where my friends shouted: "Hey Taylor, yo Tony."

The Phillies acquired Taylor in 1960 and he was given good marks as short and speedy, fielding sharply and stealing bases. He was considered the heart and soul of the Phillies through the sixties, finishing in the league's top 10 seven times for stolen bases, including six steals to home plate, a Phillies record.

Taylor played in more games at second base than any other Phillie in history.

"One of the steadiest players to ever wear a Phillies uniform," the Phillies Encyclopedia by Westcott and Frank Bilovsky proclaimed.

Dad cursed black athletes as he perched on his living room recliner watching the Phillies. Like most Philadelphians, dad's favorite target was Allen. Though Allen was one of the most gifted players to ever tread on the field, dad mockingly referred to him as "super nigger."

Dad grew up watching strong silent white ballplayers such as Williams, Ashburn, Musial and Joe DiMaggio. Dad viewed Allen as a showboat, a strutting peacock. Dad thought ballplayers should speak on the field through their play and like most white Philadelphians hated Allen's antics.

What dad didn't realize was that Allen's acting out was in part a reaction to the overt racism he had experienced in the league. Much like home run king Henry Aaron of the Atlanta Braves, who received death threats as he chased Babe Ruth's home run record, Allen and other black athletes were often jeered at by white fans around the nation, particularly in Philadelphia which had a reputation for racism.

Mom often challenged dad about his racial slurs.

"Oh, he's a nigger now," she said. "But if he hits a home run then he's a hero."

I saw it happen one afternoon at the park with dad. We were sitting on the third base side when Allen stepped to the plate.

Fans had been riding him mercilessly and today would be no different. Allen swung his mighty 40-ounce bat, missing the first pitch as the boos rose.

He swung so hard at the second pitch that he fell into the dirt. The boos got louder. Allen then knocked the third pitch out of the stadium over the center field wall as the fans and my dad rose to their feet cheering.

I was accompanying dad to Phillies games on a regular basis and the stadium was my playground. Yet the 80-year-old structure was falling into disrepair, as was the North Philadelphia neighborhood surrounding it.

The pledge by neighborhood kids to watch your car for a quarter seemed harmless when white kids were doing it decades ago. Yet it was more ominous in the '60s when drivers were confronted by black youths. With the decline of area factories, the neighborhood had grown poorer and crime-infested.

I experienced it first hand when during one game, I walked to a concession stand to get two snowballs for dad and I. On my way back, I walked down a dark stairwell, where I was followed by a young black boy about my age. As I reached the landing with my fists full, the youth stopped me and started rifling through my pockets for money. I started to cry.

"Shut the fuck up," he said.

My first reaction was to sandwich his face with the two snow cones, but I decided against it not wanting to waste the treats and knowing that I only had a penny in my pocket. By the end of 1969, though, attendance at the stadium had fallen to 520,000, the lowest since 1945.

Dad and I would usually get the ballpark in time for batting practice so I could go down to the dugouts and get autographs. One day I was eager to get into the stadium when dad tugged my hand as a huge bus pulled up to the sidewalk.

"C'mon dad," I said. "Let's go."

"Wait a minute son," he replied.

I looked up at the banner on the bus that pulled up next to us and it read "San Francisco Giants." With a whoosh, the bus doors opened and stepping off was no other than Mays, the "Say Hey Kid" himself. My baseball card collection came to life before my eyes with other Giants such as Willie McCovey and Juan Marichal following.

"Hey little man," Mays said as he tossed my hair. "Come down to the locker room after the game."

I did as I was told but a security guard wouldn't let me in. Yeah right, he said, Willie Mays told you to come down here.

I once had a chance to get Taylor's autograph. We were at the game extra early when I spotted him chatting with someone on the third base side. I ran down with my pen and game program but as I got close to the two, I chickened out, not wanting to interrupt his conversation. Taylor was speaking to his friend in Spanish

Dad saw me walk back without my trophy signature and asked what happened.

"I couldn't understand a word he said," I replied.

Connie Mack Stadium's last year was 1970. The Phillies played their last game there on Oct. 1 to a crowd of 31,822. After the game, the crowd ripped up anything they could get their hands on as souvenirs—pieces of the outfield walls, clumps of grass, anything not nailed down.

Dad attended the game and came home with a rack of three stadium chairs. Mom threw them in the basement and eventually tossed them in the trash. God, what I wouldn't give to have those chairs today to sit on my porch. A fire destroyed much of the empty stadium a year later.

The Phillies finally dealt Allen to the Cardinals in a historic trade for Curt Flood, who refused to report to the team, pointing to Philadelphia's racist attitude. Flood declared that he would not be sold as "chattel," a legal move that planted the seed of what many said would ruin the game: free agency.

Over his five years as a Philly, Allen posted numbers that could have set him on track for a trip to the Hall of Fame. He hit .300, blasted 177 home runs, knocked in another 544 runs and even stole 64 bases.

In 1971 with the team still languishing in the basement, the Phillies traded Tony Taylor to the Detroit Tigers. I was heartbroken. Our family had a party that night and my dad was sitting in the kitchen with Uncle Mick, who picked up on my somberness.

"What's wrong with the kid?" Uncle Mick asked dad.

"The Phillies traded his player today, Tony Taylor," dad said.

"Tony Taylor?" Uncle Mick barked. "Tony Taylor was a bum."

I knew that Uncle Mick was just trying to get a rise out of me, but I couldn't help it. I walked into the living room and wept.

In 1971, the Phillies finished sixth in the eastern division losing five games less than 100, a Phillies tradition. As they marched into what would be their most successful decades, they left behind baseball carnage unrivaled by any American sports team.

The close of the 1971 season meant the end of 88 years of fan frustration caused by cheap owners, a revolving door of managers, double-digit 100 loss seasons, decrepit stadiums, horrible trades and the inability to spot Hall of Fame talent. Yet through it all, the fans kept coming back.

And like most Phillies fans, even at 10-years-old, I thought I knew everything there was to know about the Phillies. But there was so much more I had to learn.

Chapter 4
The Beginning

In 1840, as baseball was just sprouting as America's pastime, Al Reach was born in London, England, the son of a cricket player. The next year Reach's family moved to Brooklyn, where he would hawk newspapers as a kid to help the family make ends meet.

When he was old enough, Reach began working 12-hour days sweating in an iron foundry. In addition to his strong work ethic, Reach had one other attribute: he was becoming an exceptional baseball player.

Only 5 feet 6, Reach started his career with the Brooklyn Eckfords, where he was good for a few hits a game. Reach made baseball history when the Philadelphia Athletics offered him $1,000 to play for them in 1865—making him the first paid professional player ever. The left-handed man who grew up in poverty jumped at the chance to play second base.

Reach helped the Athletics win the championship in 1871, the inaugural season of the first professional league, the American Association. Reach retired in 1876, becoming a sporting goods entrepreneur who made some of the league's first balls in a factory located in my Kensington neighborhood. He also had a retail store on Chestnut Street and became a millionaire.

In 1883, a man by the name of A.G. Mills was president of the young National League. To be successful, Mills knew he would need teams in America's burgeoning cities, such as New

York and Philadelphia, a city that was staking the claim as the world's greatest manufacturing center.

Philadelphia hosted the nation's 1876 centennial celebration of which one writer described the city "as cosmopolitan as Paris and as lively as Chicago." The city counted 847,000 people as its residents, boosted by the creation of railroads, shipyards and textile mills. Residents lived in two-story red brick "row" homes built by the companies for their factory workers.

"Someday their populations will be in the millions," Mills predicted.

Before the Civil War, Mills had played for the Washington Nationals and became friends with Reach. When he was looking for an owner for his Philadelphia team, he tapped his old friend for the job.

Ben Shibe, a leather expert, joined Reach as a silent partner. Shibe's name would later make its mark on Philadelphia baseball history. Col. John Rogers became the team's first general manager, a tyrannical man who worked on the governor's staff and with his bombastic personality was anything but a "silent partner."

Reach leased a tract of land in North Philadelphia that was bounded by 24th and 25th streets and Columbia and Ridge avenues, calling it Recreation Park. The field was leveled and grandstands were erected, creating the makeshift stadium that sat about 6,500 people.

To accommodate Reach, Mills moved a team called the Brown Stockings from Worcester, Mass. The squad had finished at the bottom of the league for two consecutive seasons.

If that wasn't bad enough, none of the team players made the trek to Philadelphia except two who signed with the Athletics. The Brown Stockings were so bad that only 18 people showed up at its last game.

Reach named his 1883 team the Phillies to ensure that every team in the league knew where their opponent came from. Without Brown Stockings players, the franchise assembled former minor leaguers and baseball refugees from other clubs.

The Phillies played their first game on May 1, 1883 and in

true Phillies form they lost. Before 1,200 spectators, the team flubbed a 3-0 lead in the seventh inning to lose 4-3. Statistically, their first year remains their worst percentage wise, winning 17 games and losing 81 for a .173 average. The team finished dead last, an astonishing 46 games out of first place.

One pitcher, Jack Coleman, lost 48 games. The team lost one game, 28-0, a record that still stands as the biggest shutout in league history. Reach, however, maintained hope, predicting: "Someday the Philadelphia National League club will be famous—more famous than the Athletics."

Bob Ferguson, a former Brooklyn teammate of Reach, became the first team manager but was fired after the Phillies lost 13 of their first 17 games under him. Despite their poor showing, the Phillies won five of nine games over the Athletics in an after-season exhibition series.

After the first horrendous season, Reach looked to reverse the team's fortunes, hiring one of the game's early legends, Harry Wright, as the manager. Wright coached the league's first professional team, the Cincinnati Red Stockings, in 1869. He went on to 13 seasons with winning records, managing Boston to six championships.

Reach also found the foundation of his pitching squad in Charlie Ferguson, a dominating pitcher out of Charlottesville, Va., who would become the team's first superstar. The next season the Phillies won 22 more games than their first and turned a profit of $6,083.

By 1885, the Phillies climbed to third place as Ferguson won 26 games. Ferguson also led the club in hitting with a .309 batting average and played 15 games in the outfield.

The next year, the Phillies slipped back to fourth despite having a 71-43 season that remains the third highest winning percentage in team history. The mark is only surpassed by teams in the 1970s. Ferguson won 30 games and the Phillies moved ahead of the A's in attendance showing that they were becoming the city's favorite team.

The winning ways caused Reach to build a new park. He bought another patch of North Philadelphia, this time surrounded by Broad, Huntingdon and 15th streets and Lehigh

Avenue. Though Reach called the stadium Philadelphia Baseball Park, fans referred to it as the Huntingdon Street Grounds.

The $100,000 Park, which would later become Baker Bowl, was an oddity. The distance to left and center was 400 feet while right field measured 272 feet, heaven for left-handed batters.

Consummate baseball writer Red Smith joked about the peculiar layout: "If the right fielder had eaten onions for lunch, the second baseman knew it."

Thanks to the new park, the Phillies continued to be more popular than the A's. And the team recorded another first when shortstop Billy Irwin became the first player in the league to wear a glove. The Phillies played Washington, who had an awkward, slender catcher whose name would become synonymous with Philadelphia baseball: Cornelius McGillicuddy, "Connie Mack."

The inaugural game of the stadium in 1887 ended in a 19-10 Phillies win over the New York Giants on April 30. The park, considered the finest in the country, was packed to capacity and then some with fans being forced to stand amid the crowd of 20,000.

Ferguson continued his strong pitching, winning another 22 games. But nine days after the following season began in 1888, Philadelphia lost its first sports star. Ferguson caught typhoid fever during pre-season and died on April 29. The 25-year-old ace was one game shy of 100 wins over four seasons including the first team no-hitter in 1885.

Phillies fans would not realize the depth of Ferguson's loss until decades later when they won their first league championships riding the backs of strong work horse pitchers with 20-game consecutive seasons. The Phillies finished third in1888.

A new baseball star arrived to full the Ferguson void, Sam Thompson. The strapping Indiana outfielder hit 20 home runs, the most in the National League up to that time. Thompson had hit .372 with Detroit and helped them win a title two years earlier. But the team folded and in a shrewd move, Reach immediately snapped up Thompson.

The Phillies also found a 20-year-old Irishman from Wheeling, West Virginia named Ed Delahanty. Reach paid what was considered an unfathomable sum at the time of $1,900 for Delahanty, one of five Cleveland brothers playing baseball.

The Phillies had collected a solid crop of players by 1890 that improved even more with the acquisition of "Sliding" Billy Hamilton from Kansas City. The outfield triumvirate, who would all become Hall of Famers, is still considered by some to be the greatest outfield ever assembled in baseball.

Hamilton was a textbook leadoff hitter, consistently collecting his share of hits, waiting patiently on pitches that allowed to him to gain walks and showcasing his greatest trait, stealing bases. Hamilton was most known for his head-first slides, hence the nickname.

In his first season, Hamilton hit .325 and stole 102 bases. He was even better in his second season, batting .340 with 115 steals. He led the league in batting, walks, hits, runs scored and stolen bases.

Some of the baseball writers called Hamilton "Good-eyed Bill" for his ability to screen pitches.

"He could outwait a pitcher better than any other player," one Philadelphia scribe wrote. "Good-eyed Bill had the patience of Job."

In 1892, the three outfielders each hit over .300, all standing among the league's top ten hitters. A year later, they were helped even more when the pitcher's mound was moved back from 50 feet to 60 feet six inches. Hamilton, Delahanty and Thompson led the league in hitting with marks of .380, .370 and .368.

Delahanty also led the league in home runs with 19 and runs batted in with 146.

In 1894, the Phillies fired Harry Wright, who despite his previous success couldn't pull the Phillies out of the middle of the league pack. Wright was replaced by Arthur Irwin, a former team shortstop and captain whose managerial life with the Phillies would last only two years.

Batting averages were rising and the Phillies hit .349 as a team, a major league record that still stands. And Hamilton assaulted the record books by scoring 196 runs, another major league feat that still stands.

Thompson was regularly capturing the home run crown and would collect 127, the most of any 19th century player.

A fire destroyed the Phillies Park on Aug. 6, 1894 in what seemed to be a stadium curse that they would face throughout their existence. The team played some of its games at the University of Pennsylvania fields before a new stadium opened on the former site. The park had with the first grandstands in the nation and was called by one observer the "handsomest enclosure ever devoted exclusively to outdoor athletics."

A year later in 1895, Hamilton was traded to the Boston Braves after asking for more money. The move broke up the outfield musketeers who over five seasons accumulated a collective batting average of .354. Hamilton had stolen 912 bases, a record that stood until the last half of the 20th century when Lou Brock and Rickey Henderson surpassed it. Hamilton still holds the record for scoring the most runs per game at 1.06.

Thompson retired a year later while Delahanty continued with Phillies, giving them six good seasons. Over his playing time, he knocked in more runs per game—almost one per game—than anyone.

Noted baseball writer Robert Creamer described the talented outfield as "the best outfield to ever play in the big leagues."

Despite their offensive prowess, the Phillies failed to compete for the league lead due to a problem that would become a team trademark: limp pitching. For most of the first half of the decade, the team finished with three pitchers who had double digit losses.

As the outfield broke up, the infield solidified with the 1896 arrival of Nap "Larry" Lajoie. The future Hall of Famer would become one of the greatest second baseman to ever play the game. He was literally a steal, picked up by the Phillies with another player for $1,500.

In four and half seasons with the Phillies, Lajoie never hit less than .328 with an overall batting average of .349. But one man does not a team make and the Phillies slipped to the bottom of the league again, this time under brutal manager George Stallings. Stallings tenure was short lived. He was fired in 1898 and replaced by Billy Shettsline, a 35-year old Philadelphia native who lived in Delaware County.

Shettsline was well-liked by the players and made the Phillies respectable with second and third place finishes. Writer Fred Lieb described Shettsline as "a big portly man who bubbled with good humor, good cheer and a kindly philosophy on life."

Chapter 5
A New Century

The Phillies limped into the 20th century and despite having strong bats, suffered with weak pitching and fielding, committing 125 errors—the most in the league.

In 1901, the American League was formed and the Athletics were resurrected to compete with the Phillies head to head. The A's hired Connie Mack as their manager. Former Philies partner Ben Shibe jumped ship to the Athletics, fronting the necessary money for the team to get started.

Lajoie also jumped to the Athletics after the Phillies refused to pay him $3,000, which was $600 over the league cap. The Phillies had paid Delahanty that much and Lajoie had seen one of the checks. Delahanty and Phillies outfielder Elmer Flick, another future Hall of Famer, also signed with the rival Athletics. If the Phillies could have kept the three players, analysts contended that they could have competed for the pennant, instead finishing seventh in 1902.

Saddled with marital troubles and a drinking problem, Delahanty later jumped to the Washington team in the American Association before meeting an odd fate. As the story goes, he was thrown off a train for disorderly conduct on the Canadian side of Niagara Falls and tried to stagger across a bridge but stumbled and fell into the river before being swept over the falls, never to be heard of again.

Delahanty's career average of .346 remains fourth highest of all time outdone only by Ty Cobb, Rogers Hornsby and

Shoeless Joe Jackson.

The Athletics won the pennant in 1902 and for the first time outdrew the Phillies by four to one attracting 442,000 fans.

Before the 1903 season, Reach sold the team for $170,000 to a group of investors organized by socialite James Potter. But the real news happened on Aug. 8 when a balcony in the stadium collapsed killing 12 people and injuring 300. The wreckage was equaled by the performance of the last place Phillies who lost 100 games for the first time since their formation. It would not be the last.

Through the remainder of the decade the Phillies managed to place no higher than third while the Athletics won its second pennant.

The A's, who would go on to win four pennants and three world championships over the next five years, built a new stadium six blocks down from the Phillies site. That same year, the Phillies ownership changed hands twice. The team was first purchased by city political leaders, Israel W. Durham and James P. McNichol, with banker Clarence Wolf.

They sold it for $350,000 to a former sportswriter named Harry Fogel, who had the backing of President William Taft's family. As would happen several times during their history, Fogel tried to boost the team's luck by changing its name to the "Live Wires" a moniker that fans ignored.

The Phillies luck turned around in 1911 with the hiring of Charlie "Red" Dooin. For the first time since Harry Wright, the Phillies had a consistent skipper in the former catcher who would take the Phillies into their best era to date.

The pitching staff foundation rested with a tall, sandy-haired right-handed pitcher named Grover Cleveland Alexander, who was also known as "Pete." Alexander grew up on a farm in Elba, Nebraska, where he played semi-pro ball on Sundays.

Phillies scout Patsy Rourke discovered Alexander and immediately contacted team leaders, calling Alexander the best pitching prospect he had ever seen. But the cheap Phillies gambled, not signing Alexander with hopes of picking him up in the draft. They were lucky it worked and Alexander was signed for $750.

Though the Phillies finished in fourth place, the owners and manager saw the first spark in the team in ages. Alexander won Rookie of the Year honors, winning 28 games while losing only 13. He led the league in victories, complete games, innings pitched and shutouts, the greatest performance of a pitcher to date.

With a cutting curve ball and bull's eye control, Alexander struck out 227 batters. Inquirer columnist S.O. Grauley wrote that Alexander's greatest pitching attribute was his cool demeanor.

"He was nonchalant as a side show barker, nothing worried old Pete," Grauley said. "He could fling in any pinch and he never lost his head."

Chapter 6
The First Pennant

The Phillies progress was overshadowed in 1912 when owner Fogel made unsubstantiated charges that the pennant race was fixed and umpires colluded. With yet another set of owners, former New York police commission William F. Baker took over.

The Phillies started to gel a year late in 1913 when Alexander, with his 22 wins, got help from pitching teammate Tom Seaton, who won 27 games. Another Phillies player, Gavvy Cravath, led the league in home runs with 19. Cravath would win six home run titles, hitting more than anyone to date, a position he held until the emergence of Babe Ruth.

Baker, so fond of himself, renamed the Phillies stadium Baker Bowl.

Just as the Phillies were slowly climbing out the basement, a new league was formed that rocked the National League and raided its teams. The Federal League's biggest claim from the Phillies was Seaton. The stingy Baker was unwilling to pay the pitcher more money to stay.

That same year, Baker passed on a youth coming out of Baltimore. The Orioles offered to sell him to the Phillies for $19,000. Baker replied that he would not pay for a whole league for $19,000. The player became the biggest star in the history of baseball: Babe Ruth.

When the Phillies finished sixth in the league, Baker fired Dooin and hired from within in Pat Moran. Moran was one of the first athletes in baseball who can be described as a bench coach. Though he was officially listed as a catcher, Moran spent more time sitting on the bench studying game strategy.

He was considered a solid baseball man who liked his drinks strong, a reputation that earned him the nickname "Whiskey Face." Lieb wrote that Moran had "just enough of the Irish psychic in him to give him good hunches and enable him to look through people."

Moran stressed fundamentals, making players repeat tasks considered basic baseball, such as hitting the cutoff man and turning double plays. Alexander once again carried the team on his back with 31 wins and 36 complete games. Cravath's 24 home runs stood as a new record before Ruth broke it in 1919.

To everyone's surprise, the Phillies finished in first place winning its first pennant and leading by a full seven games. They played the Red Sox with the first game being played at home in Baker Bowl. The Phillies won, 3-1, behind the ace pitching of Alexander. It would be their last World Series win in 65 years.

Alexander developed a sore arm and the Phillies lost the next four games all by one run. Fans criticized Baker for trying to make more money by putting bleachers in the outfield. Red Sox hitters hit what would normally be pop flies into the stands for home runs.

Saddened Phillies rolled a keg of beer into the locker room to try to dull the pain. Teammates carried one passed out player to a train and he didn't wake up until he reached Altoona.

The next season, the Phillies failed to repeat finishing 2 1/2 games behind the leader. Alexander again had a strong year, winning 33 including a record 16 shutouts.

"It was probably the greatest accomplishment in one season of any pitcher in the modern era," baseball historian Allen Lewis wrote.

The next season, 1917, was one of heartbreak for Phillies fans. In what is still considered the worst trade the team ever made, Baker sold Alexander to the Chicago Cubs for two players, including William "Pickles" Dillhoefer and $75,000 cash.

Baker reasoned that Alexander was going to be drafted in World War I and he wanted to dish him while his stock was hot. He later told reporters the real reason for the move.

"I needed the money."

Phillies fans were stunned. Alexander won 190 games for the Phillies, an average of 27 a year. He recorded 61 shutouts, leading the league five times. He led the league in strikeouts five times and earned run average three times. He still has the lowest earned run average of any pitcher in Phillies history.

Four years after winning a pennant, the Phillies once again were buried in the National League standings. Moran was fired the season before and while the Phillies finished 47 ½ games out of first place, Moran helped the Cincinnati Reds win the World Series. Philadelphia baseball was at rock bottom since the Athletics also finished last.

Ruth, sold by the Red Sox to the Yankees, hit an astonishing 54 home runs, ending the "dead ball" era.

Chapter 7
The Whimpering 20s

The Phillies stayed in the basement, finishing eighth for three consecutive seasons beginning in 1919. In 1922, the team lost a game to Chicago by a score of 26-23, a record that still stands as the most runs scored in a game.

"The lively ball era was now in full swing, but somehow the ball seemed livelier when a Phillies pitcher threw it," author David Jordan wrote in his 2002 Phillies history book "Occasional Glory."

Casey Stengel, a then unknown outfielder, joined the Phillies. Stengel would go on to become a baseball legend as manager of the New York Yankees.

In 1927, the Baker Bowl stands again collapsed, this time with no deaths. The incident happened due to bleacher fans stomping their feet. The stadium that was once considered premier in the league was literally crumbling. The Phillies suffered a 14-game losing streak on their way to the bottom once again. But despite the abysmal showing, 305,000 Phillies fans came to see their team.

A year later, the Phillies next superstar emerged in a humble right fielder from Fort Wayne, Ind. who the Phillies picked up once again in a steal paying him $5,000.

Chuck Klein was a welcome gust to the lack of wind that had befallen the Phillies. No one was more relieved than manager Burt Shotten.

"All right Klein, get in uniform," Shotten reportedly told his newest player. "They tell me you can hit. Goodness knows we need hitters. We need everything."

The left-handed Klein catapulted the team batting average to the league high .309. They also hit more home runs than any other team with 153 and scored an amazing 900 runs. But once again, the pitching suffered, allowing 1,032 batters to cross the plate.

Klein himself hit .356 with 43 homers and 145 runs batted in. He was in a mid-season home run streak, chasing Babe Ruth's record when Baker did something unorthodox for a home team owner. He put up a 205 foot screen atop the 40-foot wall in right field making it harder to hit home runs for left-handed batters like Klein.

Critics still contend that Baker reduced the team's home run output to stymie Klein, whose salary he would have had to match with the Ruth's. Baker dismissed the assertions, saying he was concerned about the people in the street getting him by Klein blasts. Despite Klein's power, the Phillies finished fifth in 1929 while the Athletics picked up another pennant.

In 1930, Alexander returned to the Phillies for one final season. Suffering from alcoholism and epilepsy, "Old Pete" was let go after nine games and an 0-3 record. Several years later a reporter found the Hall of Fame pitcher working for in a flea circus near Times Square.

Asked about his new career, Alexander mumbled: "It's better living off the fleas than have them live off you."

Klein posted one of his top years in 1930, batting .386 with 40 homers, 170 RBI's and a 26-game hitting streak. But again, the Phillies pitching staff was like an anchor, pulling the team down with 102 losses. The squad also finished last in fielding, a burden they would maintain for seven seasons out of the decade.

Yet the team collected a record that still stands with the Phillies of the most hits, singles, doubles, total bases, runs, RBIs and at bats. Despite the poor 52-102 win-loss record, more than 300,000 fans attended the games paying $1.10 for a box seat and 50 cents for the bleachers, where they were eager to watch the offensive explosion.

One bright spot in the season was that Baker, considered the worst owner in Phillies history, died in Montreal. He was remembered for taking a high-flying pennant team and crashing it into the basement of the league.

Chapter 8
A True Depression

By 1932 as the nation's depression truly set in, the Phillies finally won more games than they lost, 78-76, the first time in 14 years.

Klein won the Most Valuable Player award, hitting .348 and was tied with the league lead of 38 homers. Klein beat out every player in the league in hits, runs scored, slugging average and surprisingly, stolen bases. The team finished fourth.

With Baker's death the era of owner Gerald P. Nugent began. The manager, Shotton, went out on a limb and predicted the Phillies would win the 1933 pennant. How wrong he was.

The Phillies lost 92 games finishing seventh as depression-era game attendance dropped to its lowest point in 20 years at 156,500. The Phillies struggled financially once again and traded its best playcr Klein for cash.

The Phillies remained in seventh place in 1934 but welcomed a move by the state to wipe out blue laws that prohibited Sunday games. And in true Phillies fashion, the first game played on church day resulted in an 8-7 loss to the Brooklyn Dodgers.

The Phillies maintained their seventh place record in 1935, finishing last in 1936, a dishonor that also befell the city's other team, the Athletics. The combination held Philadelphia up for national ridicule as worst baseball city in America.

A huge sign on the right field wall sign promoted Lifebuoy

deoderant soap, proclaiming: "The Phillies use Lifebuoy." An irate fan scrawled underneath: "And they still stink."

The Phillies were able to get Klein back, again getting an injection of cash. Klein returned true to form, hitting .309 with 20 home runs including four in a July 10 game at Forbes Field in Pittsburgh. Klein became the fourth player in baseball history to reach the mark and second Phillie next to Ed Delahanty.

The team remained at the bottom of the league for the rest of the decade. In 1938, the well-worn Baker Bowl was decomposing. The team had played there for 51 ½ years and the stadium that once shone as the brightest athletic field in the nation was referred to as "the toilet bowl" and "the cigar box."

The Phillies left the stadium, entering a deal with the Athletics to share Shibe Park. The new arrangement didn't help the team's fortunes as they lost 104 games in 1938, starting a string of five consecutive last place finishes and 100 loss seasons.

The year was also the arrival of a young Texan broadcaster named Byrum "By" Saam. Saam gave the radio play-by-play for both the Phillies and the Athletics and his crisp voice would become the signal of summer in Philadelphia.

In their final season of the decade, the Phillies finished in the basement an astonishing 50 ½ games out of first place. The team led the league in all the wrong categories: batting, pitching and fielding.

New manager Doc Prothro got a chance to see his motley crew in Spring Training, calling them "the worst looking crowd of ballplayers in big league uniforms I've ever seen."

The team even let Klein go before letting him return for a final season in 1940 when he hit an anemic .218 with seven home runs.

Chapter 9
Bombs Away

With World War II about to escalate with the bombing of Pearl Harbor, wartime baseball would not be kind to Philadelphia. The Phils and A's would both finish in the baseball cellar six times in the decade with the Phillies drawing half the number of fans as their inter-city counterparts.

In 1941, the team lost 111 games, a team record that has yet to be broken.

After 1942 and finishing an amazing 62 ½ games out of first, the Phillies once again tried to alter their name simply to the "Phils" in hopes of getting a fresh start. Team owners also didn't want the baseball squad being confused with the popular cigar brand named Phillies.

The switch never took, ignored by fans who despite suffering consecutive losing seasons remained devoted. Describing a short winning streak in 1942, Phillies second baseman and future legendary Pittsburgh manager Danny Murtaugh said: "It might be a cause for a congressional investigation. They probably thought the opponent was throwing games. I know it's hard to look back and wonder how any club could be that bad, but we were."

During one Phillies game, only 400 fans showed up at Shibe Park in a year that gained them the infamous National League record of having lost over 100 games in five straight seasons.

In 1943, the National League took over the financially struggling Phillies. With Nugent debts over $300,000, league turned over the team to William Cox, a former New York businessman and sportsman.

The Phillies financial situation was so bad at one point during the dire times that it reportedly sold its office furniture to pay for Spring Training. Cheap road hotels with phone booth rooms were the norm. "You had to go in the hall to change your mind," Kirby Higbe, a Phillies pitcher from 1939 and 1940, told reporters.

The story goes that at one time in the 1920s, the team was so broke that it couldn't pay its groundkeepers and rented three goats, kept under the left field stands, to help keep the grass from growing.

The change in ownership helped the Phillies win 64 games, their best record in eight years. But that still didn't stop them from earning more embarrassment. Cox was banned from baseball after acknowledging that he bet $25 to $100 on Phillies games.

When the team situation seemed like it could get no worse, a white knight arrived to rescue the Phillies. His name was Robert M.J. Carpenter Jr. The millionaire made his money from the DuPont chemical company in nearby Wilmington, Del. and bought the team for his 28-year old son for $400,000. With sizable money now serving as a foundation for the club, young Carpenter would lead the Phillies out of the basement.

The turnaround wouldn't come quick. The Phillies finished last in both 1944 and 1945, when they lost 108 games and finished at the bottom in batting, fielding, extra base hits, home runs, earned run average and complete games. Throw in a 16-game losing streak and you have one abysmal 1945 season.

The team once again tried to change its name in hopes of improving its luck. This time, Carpenter had a fan contest to come up with the best nickname. After receiving 5,064 entries, Carpenter chose the winner as the "Blue Jays."

Students at Johns Hopkins University in Baltimore revolted. The college nickname, used for 68 years, was the Blue Jays and the students immediately passed a resolution that the Phillies use of their name "is a reprehensible act which brings disgrace and dishonor to the good name of Johns Hopkins University."

Again, the Phillies name change never caught on with the fans.

In 1946, the Phillies began their march to a second pennant. Carpenter instructed team leaders to build from within, through their farm system. The first year, Carpenter brought up Del Ennis, a slugging left fielder who grew up in the city's Olney section and quickly became a fan favorite. The 20-year-old Ennis clobbered the competition in the military league in the Pacific. Also brought up was catcher Andy Seminick.

Ennis began doing in the majors what he did in the military, hitting home runs and driving runners home. He would become the greatest run producer on the Phillies to date, even better than Klein and Delahanty.

Ennis hit .313 with 17 home runs as a rookie and earned Rookie of the Year honors. Fans came to see their new young players and the Phillies exceeded the 1 million mark in attendance, the largest crowds in three decades. And this despite the Phillies finishing fifth, their highest finish in 14 years.

In 1947, the National League broke the color barrier with the arrival of Jackie Robinson to the Dodgers. Robinson's first visit to Philadelphia was memorable for all the wrong reasons. For being black, Robinson was turned away from staying at the Ben Franklin Hotel where the rest of the team was staying.

Phillies General Manager Herb Pennock warned Dodgers GM Branch Rickey not to bring Robinson to Philly. "You just can't bring that nigger here with the rest of your team, Branch," Pennock reportedly warned. "We're just not ready for that sort of thing."

Ready or not, Robinson showed up at Shibe Park in a game that was forever etched in his memory. Phillies manager Ben Chapman taunted Robinson from the dugout, pitching racial slurs his way. Chapman used terms derogatory to blacks, making references to such things as thick lips and large skulls. Chapman even had the gall to warn other Dodger players that they would pick up a disease for playing with Robinson.

Robinson called it the most unpleasant day in his life. It "brought me nearer to cracking up than I ever had been," Robinson told reporters. Robinson stayed cool but inside was churning.

He later said that he wanted to "throw down my bat, stride over to the Phillies dugout, grab one of those white son of bitches and smash his teeth with my despised black fist."

Chapman dismissed the incident as his way of trying to knock Robinson off his game. Rattling opponents was as old as baseball and Chapman was only seeing if Robinson could take it, he said.

The largest crowd in Shibe Park history to date—41,660 fans—paid to see Robinson and the doubleheader with the Dodgers.

The Phillies tables turned in 1948 with the arrival of Ashburn as the center fielder and Roberts as the pitcher. Both came up through the Phillies farm system while the Phillies picked up Dick Sisler in a trade with St. Louis.

Pennock, the man who built the team, would never see its fruition, dying in 1948 from a cerebral hemorrhage, a crippling blow to the organization.

Ashburn, a 21-year-old Nebraskan who was 5 feet 10, set a new league rookie record by hitting in 23 straight games and compiling a .333 batting average. He also stole a league leading 32 bases and won Rookie of the Year honors. Ashburn was described as aggressive, competitive and intense and was being compared to Sliding Bill Hamilton, arguably the greatest lead off hitter in Phillies history.

Ennis hit 30 home runs, the most since Klein 16 years earlier. But the chief acquisition came in the managing department with the hiring of Eddie Sawyer. The 37-year-old biology teacher had coached Phillies farm clubs in Toronto and Utica, N.Y. and was accustomed to working with young players.

The usually reserved Sawyer fired up his team in August 1949 when he accused them of playing lackadaisical. He was tired of watching players eat lobster and enjoying the high life that good salaries provided ballplayers.

The lashing worked. The Phillies won three games from the eventual pennant winning Dodgers. The team won 16 of their last 26 games, giving the team a third place finish, the highest slot since 1917.

A bizarre incident occurred that year involving Phillies first baseman Eddie Waitkus, who was picked up from the Cubs. While the Phillies played Chicago, Waitkus was summoned to a hotel room where a woman obsessed with him shot him in the chest with a .22 caliber rifle, the bullet almost shattering his spine. Ruth Anne Steinhagen, was upset that the Cubs had traded Waitkus.

The 19-year-old stenographer was found to have a shrine in her room dedicated to the ballplayer. She was put into a mental institution. Waitkus' tale became legendary, serving as the foundation of the 1952 book "The Natural," which was later made into a classic baseball movie starring Robert Redford.

As the Phillies marched into 1950 and their second pennant, the team dug themselves out of a 32-year span of futility in which they finished last 16 times and played for 16 different managers. Their worst period came between 1938 and 1942 when they not only finished last every season but lost 100 games.

Yet the true golden era for the Philadelphia Phillies would not come for another 25 years.

Chapter 10
Renovation

Veterans Stadium made its debut in 1971. The gigantic $52 million concrete bowl held 56,000 in South Philadelphia and rivaled similar stadiums in Pittsburgh, St. Louis and Cincinnati.

The space-age looking stadium was built to accommodate both football and baseball and we were excited that our Phillies were finally going to play on astroturf, the fake grass that was the rage in other team stadiums. The greatest feature for us, though, was that the seats at the top of the stadium—the nose bleeds as people called them would sell for a mere 50 cents.

Unlike the more intimate Connie Mack Stadium, Phillies players looked like ants on the Veterans Stadium field from the high seats. The sight lines were terrible.

The Phillies even had new uniforms that debuted the year before. The blue cosmic suits contained a new "P" with a baseball in it over the heart that looked like softball uniforms.

With the new stadium came a new roster. Players like Greg Luzinski, a beefy slugger from Chicago, and Larry Bowa, a feisty shortstop from California, took the field along with catcher Bob Boone, another California product. The crew was part of a Phillies farm system that in 1968 was voted tops in the league.

My book covers at school featured the new Phillies roster with photos of players such as Bowa and his second base partner, Denny Doyle. The team even had new announcers with Harry Kalas, whose legendary voice would eventually become the signature for the Philadelphia-based NFL Films, teaming up with Ashburn, who was the color analyst and one of the most knowledgeable baseball men around.

None of the changes had an impact on the performance of the team, which lost 95 games in 1971 and finished last in the six-team division. But the Phils did set an attendance record of 1.5 million fans who came out to see the new park.

The highlight of the year came on June 23 in Cincinnati when pitcher Rick Wise threw a no-hitter against the powerful Cincinnati Reds. Wise allowed only one base runner through a walk and the pitcher himself even hit two home runs.

I remember playing on the streets of our row house Kensington neighborhood in East Philadelphia and listening to the game through the window screen of my pal, Butchy Sullivan. Most nights you could stroll along the sidewalk and hear By Saam's play-by-play radio broadcast of the Phillies emanating through open windows. But this night, everyone was leaning next to the window screens, cheering each painstaking out as Wise approached his feat.

As if pitching a no-hitter wasn't drama enough, Wise had to face Pete Rose for the final out. Rose was arguably the greatest hitter to ever play the game and we considered him a son of a bitch. As we all tensed up for the final out, the neighborhood was silent until Rose lined out to third baseman John Vukovich as we kids all jumped jubilantly around as if we had won the pennant and Philadelphia let out a collective cheer.

So it was a shock in 1972 when the Phillies traded Wise for an unknown Cardinals pitcher named Steve Carlton. Both Wise and Carlton were unhappy with their contracts so the teams just swapped their problems.

Phillies fans worried that we were making another Fergie Jenkins trade. Carlton was considered a flake who strengthened his pitching arm by grinding it into a bag of brown rice. He also studied wine and practiced eastern religions.

It was the year that Bob Carpenter turned the reigns of the team over to his son, Ruly, a former Yale football player and baseball captain. The young Carpenter immediately promoted Paul Owens, known as the Pope for his resemblance to Pope Paul VI, to general manager. Owens had planted the splendid farm system, now he was going to get the chance to harvest his baseball crops.

The Phillies were awful again. They won 59 games losing 97 and scored fewer runs than any team in the league. The team ended 37 ½ games out of first place. But something interesting happened on the way to the basement. Carlton won 27 games, losing 10 and winning the Cy Young Award for best pitcher. He won almost half of the team's games, an accomplishment unseen in baseball at the time.

Carlton had a paralyzing slider that was a joy to watch break from the center field television cameras.

"Hitting Steve Carlton was like trying to drink coffee with a fork," Pittsburgh Pirates slugger Willie Stargell once told reporters.

Other good signs surfaced. The powerful Luzinski, known as "The Bull," hit .281 with 18 home runs and 68 runs batted in. Bowa, the scrawny shortstop, led the league in triples with 13. And in September, the Phillies called up from their minor league system an unknown red-haired, mustached man who arguably would become the greatest Phillie to ever wear the uniform: Michael Jack Schmidt.

Schmidt was originally a shortstop who turned off other teams because of a minor knee injury. But Phillie scout Tony Lucadello, who had discovered Fergie Jenkins, was impressed by Schmidt, ironically calling him the next Jim Fregosi.

"Wiry, raw-boned, can drive the ball," Lucadello's report said. "Quick bat, soft hands, good range."

The Phillies improved 12 games in 1973 over the previous season even though they remained in last place. They had a new manager in Danny Ozark, a droopy-eyed Los Angeles Dodgers coach, who like pennant-winning Pat Moran almost 60 years earlier, preached fundamentals. Despite its poor performance, the Phillies still attracted 1.4 million loyal fans.

That same year, Tony Taylor hit .303 helping the Tigers win the American League eastern division. Every morning, I would rush to my step to retrieve the newspaper to read about Taylor's pinch-hit heroics. Detroit's sportswriters dubbed him "Tony the Tiger" and my Uncle Mick was nowhere to be found.

The next year, 1974, Taylor returned to the Phillies as a free agent, now wearing No. 12. He got regular standing ovations from the fans and the team held an appreciation night for him, showering him with gifts.

"It's almost impossible to find the perfect love affair," the Phillies Encyclopedia said. "Tony Taylor and the fans of Philadelphia came as close as you could."

The Phillies almost broke .500, winning 80 games and going from sixth to third. Second baseman Dave Cash introduced the slogan "Yes We Can" and Philadelphia fans started to believe. The biggest change came in Schmidt, who during his rookie year in 1973 hit a paltry .196 with 136 strikeouts. A year later, he blossomed banging 36 home runs to lead the league while attendance was crawling higher to 1.8 million.

By 1975 the Phillies were legitimate contenders for the first time in 11 years and the '64 collapse. The team went 86-76 finishing second behind the Pirates. Ozark was platooning players, making household names out of prankster outfielder Jay Johnstone and "Downtown" Ollie Brown, both of whom hit over .300.

The year also marked the return of Richie Allen, who now wanted to be referred to as Dick Allen. Allen told the Chicago White Sox that he planned to retire. He had won the American League Most Valuable Player award in 1972 when he batted .308, hit 37 home runs and knocked in 113. The Sox decided to trade him to the Atlanta Braves.

Allen being Allen, he refused to report, saying that he would not play in the deep South again. But surprisingly, he agreed to return to the Phillies after being prompted by Schmidt, Cash and Ashburn. He got a standing ovation at his first at bat in which he singled.

With his farm system recruits playing like All-Stars, Owens decided to beef up the roster with two critical acquisitions. The first was relief pitcher Tug McGraw, who had pitched with the Mets since 1965, including on their surprising "Amazing Mets" World Championship team of 1969. Up to his arrival to the Phillies, McGraw was best known as the soul of the 1973 Mets team that won the pennant following Tug's motto "You Gotta'

Believe."

The other pickup was Garry Maddox, the center fielder and heir apparent to Willie Mays in San Francisco. The Vietnam veteran was solid both at the bat and on the field. Baseball great Ralph Kiner once told radio listeners that two-thirds of the earth was covered by water, the other third by Maddox.

With a solid team in place, the Phillies were about to embark on the golden period of their history.

Chapter 11
The Bicentennial

In 1976, the bicentennial was celebrated in Philadelphia, which also hosted the All-Star game.

The Phillies had languished in the back of the pack for so long that it didn't seem real that they were gliding in first place with a commanding 10-game lead over the Pirates. They were staring at their first playoff appearance in 26 years.

In what may be viewed as the game that turned the franchise around, the Cubs rocked Carlton on April 18 taking a 13-2 lead at Wrigley Field. Yet the Phillies stormed back with Schmidt hitting an incredible four home runs to help the Phils win by a football score of 18-16 in 10 innings. The game would become known in Phillies history as "the slugfest in Chicago."

The Phillies won 50 of their first 70 games and held a 15 ½ game lead in late August. But in true Phillies fashion, the club scared the fans by dropping 12 of 13 in three weeks as their lead shrunk to three games, resurrecting the ghosts of 1964.

But like a pilot getting his dovetailing plane back on track, the Phils launched a winning streak of 13 out of 16 to capture the division title with 101 victories, the most in Phillies history.

Schmidt again led the league in home runs with 38 and Luzinski added 21 while Carlton posted another 20-game season losing only seven and Ozark was named Manager of the Year by The Sporting News.

Allen started his sulking again, this time complaining about playing time. His most visible protest came when the team celebrated capturing the Eastern Division crown with a 4-1 win over the Montreal Expos sending them to the playoffs for the first time since 1950. Cameras zoomed in on Allen sitting alone in the dugout after the win as the other players celebrated in the locker room.

The Phils had had enough of Allen and released him at the end of the year, bringing the 12-year Allen period with the Phillies to an end.

During his 15-year baseball career, Allen batted .292, hit 351 homers and knocked in more than 1,000 runs. But he would be remembered most throughout the league for his trouble making.

Despite their success in the regular season, the Phillies were swept in three games by the explosive Big Red Machine, the Cincinnati Reds. In his book, however, Fitzpatrick reported that a prophetic moment occurred in the Reds dugout during the series. Rose looked over at the Phillies and said to fellow team member Joe Morgan: "That team's got a lot of talent. All they need is a leader."

Phillies scholars still call the 1977 Phillies the best in franchise history. They again won 101 games tying the team record of a year before and Carlton won his second Cy Young Award with a 23-10 record. Luzinski finished second in MVP voting by batting .309 with 39 homers and 130 runs batted in.

The league championship series was tied at one game apiece on Oct. 7 when Dodger pitcher Burt Hooten took the mound. The young pitcher started having control problems and Phillies fans, smelling blood, pounced on him. The 63,700 sitting in the concrete bowl began "hooting" at Hooten.

"I don't think I've ever heard noise like that," Bowa later told reporters. "They hooted him right off the mound."

The Phillies led 5-3 heading into the 9th inning in a game that would later be forever remembered as "Black Friday." Ozark failed to substitute Jerry Martin for Luzinski in left field for defensive purposes as he had been doing. Dodger Manny Mota hit a shot that bounced off the lumbering Luzinski's glove, knocking in a run.

The game became more bizarre when a shot caromed off

44

Schmidt and Bowa picked up the ball and by all accounts of everybody watching, threw the runner out at first. But the umpire called him safe. A subsequent wild pick-off throw followed and the Dodgers collected three runs in the inning to win the game, 6-5.

The game ranks with the 1964 skid as one of the Phillies greatest disasters. Owens would call it "probably one of the worst days of my career."

The following night, 65,000 Phillies fans, including my dad and brother, Dan, braved a steady rain in a game that should have never been played because of the weather conditions. With television networks having invested heavily in broadcasting the primetime game, National League President Chub Feeney allowed it to continue. The Phillies lost 4-1.

The argument could be made that the Dodgers had to play in the same conditions as the Phillies but as fans, we couldn't help but to think that the baseball gods were against us once again.

We were confronted with the dilemma: is it better to languish in the basement so that your hopes were not dashed or race for the finish line, then be disappointed? I had to admit that as a fan, the playoff excitement and tension was addicting and our city was electrified.

But I couldn't help thinking that the Phillies were leading our city into the desert and offering us a cup of water, pulling it back just as we were ready to quench our 94-year thirst for one world championship.

Chapter 12
A World Championship

The Phillies finished in first place of the eastern division for the third year in a row in 1978, though they won 11 fewer games.

Knee and hamstring injuries sidelined Schmidt, who fans accused of being soft. One of my most embarrassing moments as a Phillies fan was watching Schmidt get booed. Phillies fans were known across the nation as the "boo birds" for their incessant booing of the city football team, The Philadelphia Eagles. But booing the man who was arguably the greatest third baseman to ever play the game was a stretch, even for Phillies fans.

Future Phillies manager Jim Fregosi would explain the source of Philadelphia booing: fans took pride in their city and the team that represented them across the nation.

"Fans in Philly are like an extra coach," Fregosi told the press. "If they see a guy not running out a grounder, they'll boo the hell out of him. The coach doesn't have to say a thing."

The Philadelphia sportswriters were just as merciless.

"Philadelphia is the only city where you can experience the thrill of victory and the agony of reading about the next day," Schmidt told reporters.

Carlton had long stopped talking to the Philadelphia media, calling them "poison."

"As far as I'm concerned," he told the writers. "The press is one of the biggest enemies you have."

Luzinski bulled his way through 1978, again pounding 35

homers. Many were into the yellow seats in the upper deck, which seemed just below heaven. They remain some of the longest shots recorded in the stadium. We all thrilled at the thought that Luzinski or Pirates slugger Stargell would someday knock the ball out of the stadium like players regularly did at Connie Mack. But to do it at Veterans Stadium was impossible, not that Luzinski didn't try.

Luzinski had hit 29 homers or more in each of four seasons making it to the All-Star game as many times.

The Phillies headed into the playoffs beating the Pittsburgh Pirates for the division title in the last weekend yet again faced the dreaded Los Angeles Dodgers for the pennant. Despite playing the first two games at home, the Phils fell behind two games to none before their fans who arrived to cheer but left booing. The team rallied for a 9-4 victory in the third game held in L.A. behind the pitching of Carlton, who with Luzinski also hit a home run.

Game 4 in Los Angeles resulted in a 3-3 struggle going into the ninth. Many of us believed that if the Phils could win game four, they would return to Philly and win the pennant in Game 5. But in the bottom of the 10th with two outs, the sure-handed Garry Maddox, nicknamed "The Minister of Defense" and considered the best center fielder in the game at the time, dropped a soft line drive hit by Dusty Baker that set up the winning run. The shot put another dagger into the hearts of Phillies fans everywhere.

Afterward, Maddox refused to make excuses to reporters.

"The ball was right in my glove," he said. "It was not a tough play, just a routine line drive. It's something I'll never forget the rest of my life."

As a fan, it was hard to get on Maddox, who was one of the steadiest Phillies in recent memory.

In 1979, the Phillies were forced to take a good long, hard look in the mirror. They needed a spark and found it in their former nemesis Rose. The three-time batting champion who would eventually take root at first base. Just his presence caused park attendance to soar to record levels of 2.8 million.

When we played the Reds, Pete Rose was a son of a bitch,

now he was our son of a bitch. The high school dropout with the Prince Valient haircut knew one thing about baseball: how to win.

"He wanted to win so damn bad," pitcher Ron Reed told reporters. "That he infected everyone on the team."

He had guided the Reds to four pennants and two World Series. Ashburn summed up the winning ways of Rose best in an interview with the Philadelphia Evening Bulletin.

"If you're looking for the secret to Pete Rose's success, it would be his ability to concentrate, the ability to shut out everything else, his personal problems, the cheers, the boos," Ashburn said. "When Rose steps into the baseball world, all other worlds are left behind."

Rose ranked second in the league the previous year with a .331 average. Team owner Ruly Carpenter initially refused to get into a bidding war for Rose. Carpenter hated the free agent system and was prophetic in claiming that baseball world championships would go to the teams who paid the most. New York Yankees owner George Steinbrenner had proven the case, winning championships in 1977 and 1978 with free agents Reggie Jackson and Catfish Hunter, both from the Oakland A's.

But Carpenter, who was said to have a reported fortune of $330 million, signed Rose to a four-year $3.2 million pact that made the Phillies the highest paid team in baseball.

Despite the Phillies having three potential Hall of Famers in Rose, Schmidt and Carlton, the team languished finishing fourth at 14 games out of first place with 84 wins and 78 losses. Schmidt, who credited Rose with helping to deal with pressure, returned to form hitting 45 home runs and Rose added his .331 average with a career high 20 stolen bases.

Watching "Charlie Hustle" play ball was sheer joy. I remember one night going out to the park to see the Phils play their in-state rival Pittsburgh Pirates. Pirates outfielder Al Oliver had singled and was standing at first when the next batter hit a sharp grounder right past Rose. The ball went by so fast that Rose began acting like it was a pop fly calling for the ball in the air. The confused Oliver stood at first base while the right fielder picked up the ball and threw to second for the force out. Classic baseball.

But the Phillies struggle caused Owens to fire Ozark in late August. Despite leading the Phillies to three divisional titles, Ozark couldn't get them to the promised-land. Fans didn't help, regularly chanting "Oze Must Go" at Phillies games. Owens hired farm director Dallas Green as the team skipper.

In 1980, Phillies fans were voted by the players as the noisiest, most supportive and most hostile. Going into the season, Bowa felt the pressure to finally deliver the prize.

"We had the label of choke artists," he told reporters.

Schmidt agreed, telling the media: "If you were a Philly kind of guy, someone who always had dirt on their uniform like Pete, those fans were the best in baseball. But if they saw something that suggested that you didn't care, they'd carve you up."

The team sold 18,000 season tickets for the year, second only to the Dodgers. On opening night, 48,500 came to watch Carlton tame the nemesis Montreal Expos, 4-1.

The new manager, Dallas Green, coached the team into playing more "we than I" hanging a banner with the phrase in the clubhouse. Though players like Carlton and Schmidt collected Cy Young Awards and home run crowns, the team had not benefited.

Some players, like Luzinski, disliked the feisty Green, who was once described "as subtle as a crowbar." Luzinski called him "Hitler" and joined other players in criticizing the amount of playing time they were getting.

The team offered no indication that they would be able to live up to their hype. But again they rolled into June on the back of Carlton, who had 10 of the team's 24 wins. By the All-Star break, they were 41-35, good enough to be behind the Expos by a game.

The season, and the Phillies fortunes, changed on Aug. 10 after the team lost four games to the Pirates. Between a Sunday double-header, Green ripped into his team in a closed door meeting that Daily New sports writer Bill Conlin said could be "heard through bolted steel doors."

"I lit into them pretty good," Green told the Inquirer's Carchidi. "They were talking the talk but not walking the walk. I accused them of being too cool. That was part of the agenda, everyone wanted to be Mr. Cool like Mike Schmidt."

For his part, on Sept. 1, Owens laid down the law, challenging the players to fight him before a game in San Francisco. Owens planted the seeds of the Phillies team, nurturing players like Schmidt, Luzinski and Bowa while adding to its development by dealing for others like McGraw, Maddox and Rose.

"You don't like this, come knock on my door," Owens told the team. "I'm in room 413, I 'm 56 years old and you may knock me down but I'll get back up...I'll keep coming back until you sons of bitches understand that you're a good ballclub."

The lashings worked. The Phillies turned things around in September playing to Green's motto: "grind it out." They posted a 23-11 record in September, winning 19 of their last 25. But during a stretch of games at home with Chicago, Bowa ripped into fans booing calling us the "worst fans in the world, front-running motherfuckers."

Conlin took to the city's defense. "How can you front run in a town which claims two National League pennants in a century that is four-fifths gone?" The Phillies won a critical Sept. 29 game that was decided in a 15th inning rally when they scored three runs against the Cubs, showing the team had heart.

McGraw gave up only three runs in 52 1/3 innings after July 17. He called himself "The Tylenol Kid" because he was taking eight aspirins daily to heal his sore arm.

If Rose was the team leader, McGraw was its heart and soul. He had experienced winning with the Mets and brought a quirky humor to the locker room. He named his pitches, such as his fastball, which was a "John Jameson" named for Irish Whiskey. "The Titanic" was his sinker while his "Bo Derek" had a nice tail on it and his "Cutty Sark" sailed. Home run pitches were labeled "Sinatra balls" in reference to the song "Fly Me To The Moon."

Reporters once asked McGraw how he compared playing on

real grass versus Astro Turf: "I never smoked Astro Turf," he said.

When asked by reporters what he intended to do with his share of the 1969 World Series money, Tug said: "Ninety percent I'll spend on good times, women and Irish whiskey, the other 10 percent I'll probably waste."

The Phils also got an unexpected boost from rookie pitcher, Marty Bystrom, who came up at the end of the season and went 5-0. The team finished dead even with Montreal for the division title that was decided in a final three-game series in Canada.

Schmidt won the title almost single handily by winning the first game on a Friday night with a homer. That was followed on Saturday by an 11-inning nail biter which ended when Schmidt launched a two-run homer to capture a 6-4 victory, giving the team its fourth division crown in five years.

The five-game National League Championship Series with the Houston Astros was considered one of the finest ever played. Before a record crowd of 65,280, the Phillies took a quick one-game lead behind the solid pitching of Carlton and a two-run homer by Luzinski.

Houston tied the series in the second game, winning 7-4 and giving them home field advantage in the final three games to be played in the cursed Houston Astrodome, where the Astros dominated. True to form, the Astros grabbed game three 1-0 in 11 innings to take a 2 to 1 lead. In game four, the Phillies were held scoreless for seven innings, bringing their scoreless inning streak in the series to 17 as they fell behind 2-0.

Philadelphia was on the verge of heartbreak yet again. But the Phils scored three runs in the seventh to go ahead, 3-2. Houston tied it in the bottom of the ninth, sending the series into extra innings yet again. The Phillies scored two runs in the top of the 10th, the crucial winning run coming off a Luzinski double that Pete Rose scored on by slamming Astros catcher Bruce Bochy with a forearm to the head at home plate for a 5-3 victory.

"I know Pete Rose," said Rose's former Reds cohort Morgan. "Pete Rose was never going to stop."

The crucial fifth game is remembered as one of the greatest playoff games ever. The legendary Houston strikeout king and consummate fastball pitcher Nolan Ryan had a 5-2 lead when the Phillies came to bat in the top of the eighth inning. Ryan was an astonishing 112-3 when leading after seven innings. Prospects looked grim as we sat on the edge of our chairs, staring at the television.

"For the Phillies, October isn't a month," wrote the Daily News' Ray Didinger. "It's a padded cell waiting to slam shut on them."

But the Phillies scored five in the eighth to take the lead only to see Houston answer with two in the bottom of the inning. That sent the game into extra innings for the third time in the series. The Phillies won their third pennant in 97 years in the 10th inning when Maddox hit a double, driving in the winning run as Phillies pitcher Dick Ruthven shut down Houston hitters in the bottom of the inning to protect the lead and secure the win. It translated into the Phillies first trip to the World Series in 30 years. And it was fitting that the final out of the game was caught by Maddox.

The Phillies World Series challengers, The Kansas City Royals, took the same road to the championship as the Phils. Kansas City had gotten into the American League pennant series three times—1976, 1977 and 1978—never able to make it to the World Series.

The Phils, now dubbed "The Team That Wouldn't Die," won the first two games of the series, their first World Series win in 65 years since 1915.

George Brett, the Royals hitting ace who played a similar role as the team leader like Rose, was sidelined in the first two games by flaring hemorrhoids. Brett played the third game, joking that "the pain is behind me." He made a difference. Kansas City won the next two games, 4-3 and 5-3 to tie the series. The closeness of the matches meant that the Phillies had played in 13 consecutive games decided by two runs or less. Talk about tension.

The Phillies won Game 5, 4-3, with McGraw being credited with the win. In one of the most memorable scenes of the series, the Royals Hal McRae hit a bottom of the 9th inning foul with two on and one out into the left field stands that looked like it was headed toward being a homer. The ball hooked foul and all of America saw McGraw standing on the pitcher's mound putting his hand underneath his shirt and flapping it over his heart. The Phils held on and were headed home with a one-game lead.

In Game 6, Carlton took the mound before 65,800 Veterans Stadium fans eager to see their team win their first championship in the 97-year history of the franchise, the longest drought in baseball history at the time. The Phils led 4-1 going into the eighth inning when McGraw loaded the bases putting every Phillies fan into panic that the team would somehow find a way to drop victory yet again. He got out that jam only to get into a similar dilemma in the ninth when he again loaded the bases.

In one of the plays that will go down in Phillies history, the Royals Frank White hit a pop fly in front of the Phillies dugout. Boone waddled under it, seemingly to make the easy play. Then the unimaginable happened. The ball popped out of his glove. Yet standing right next to him was Rose, ever the fundamentalist playing backup, who caught the ball for the second out of the inning and brought the Phillies one out closer to the championship. It was as if the Phillies had picked up Rose the year before just to be standing there for that play.

But as one sportswriter wrote: "There wasn't a person in the stadium, in the city, in all of baseball who didn't believe that the home team remained capable of blowing this lead, this game and this series."

Memorable Phillies moments never occurred in Philadelphia. They won their first two pennants in Boston and Brooklyn and even captured this flag in Houston. They won their four national league east titles in Chicago, Pittsburgh and twice in Montreal.

As fans, we were glued to our television sets as Willie Wilson strolled to the plate for what could be the final out. I was at a party at the house of my friend George Post, a diehard Phillies fan since World War II and a foreman at the nearby

Schmidt's brewery. We loved to watch the games at the Post house because George would get so wound up. We would be able to sit in his kitchen and keep score of the game based on the shouts coming from the living room.

A raucous "yeah" meant the Phillies had scored while a shriek of "Jesus Christ!" was a run for the opponents. Three Jesus Christs to one yeah meant we were down three to one.

We all huddled around the television when Wilson was behind two strikes. All of America witnessed the Philadelphia police taking the fields holding menacing German Shepherd dogs on tight leashes near the grandstands to prevent any rioting. This was the town of former police commissioner and Mayor Frank Rizzo, who once said he could invade Cuba and win with his police department. There was going to be no trouble in big Frank's town.

McGraw would later tell sports writers how when he began warming up the bullpen he had to retrieve his glove from under the chin of one of the dogs, who was slobbering all over it. On the center field electronic scoreboard were the words: "Lord, this is heaven!"

McGraw winded up, delivered the pitch and Wilson swung through it, giving Philadelphia its first World Championship. McGraw leaped from the pitcher's mound with his arms stretched to the heavens as if signaling a touchdown.

He would later call it the slowest fastball he ever threw.

"It took 97 years to get there," he quipped.

Fans across the city erupted in hugs, laughter and danced in the streets. It was like New Year's Eve, as people poured from their houses, banging pots and pans or drove around the neighborhood in cars, beeping their horns, riding on the hoods and waving Phillies banners.

We began wandering the streets looking for an assembly point and found it outside the Chug-a-Mug tavern. Dozens of people stood on the sidewalk or in the middle of the street spraying each other with quarts of beer, the working man's champagne. A backhoe came rolling down the street. As we all tried to jump up on it, I slipped and was headed under the giant wheels before my pal, Joe Quigley, pulled me to safety.

McGraw would later put the championship in the best perspective in talking to reporters: "That guy sitting up in the 700 level in center field who started going to games with his great-grandfather and his grandfather and father and all those year of frustration and then all of a sudden, the Phillies win a world championship. I think it meant more to him."

McGraw was talking about us. At nearby Kensington and Allegheny avenues, fans burned an effigy of George Brett from the scaffolding of the elevated trains.

"These were people for whom sitting on the front steps on a sweltering summer night, drinking a cold Schmidt's and listening to By Saam broadcast a Phillies game was sacred tradition," Fitzpatrick wrote.

It was the most watched World Series in history and even Bowa, who had earlier in the year derided fans, was now making peace.

"That was the greatest moment of my life," he told the media. "And I'm glad to share it with the greatest fans in baseball."

The following day, 2 million Phillies fans lined Broad Street for the victory parade. Flatbed trailers rolled slowly down the city's longest thoroughfare through the cheering masses as rose petals were spotted stuck to the tears rolling down the face of Owens, the team architect.

McGraw became a city folk hero and before 90,000 fans waiting for the victory rally at JFK Stadium, hoisted a copy of the Daily News in the air with a headline proclaiming: "We Win!"

"All through baseball history, Philadelphia has had to take a backseat to New York City," McGraw told the crowd over the public address system. "But New York City can take this world championship and stick it!"

Thunderous roars echoed from South Philly. In the postseason, Schmidt won the National League MVP award after batting .286 with a Phillies record 48 homers and 121 runs batted in. He was the first Phillie to win the award since Jim Konstanty in 1950. Meanwhile, Carlton, who went 24-8, won his third Cy Young Award.

The Phillies won the first half of the strike plagued 1981 season but lost in the fifth game of a five game series with the Montreal Expos in a split-season playoff match. The team traded fan favorite Greg Luzinski to Chicago in a cold blooded way.

"I love Greg," Green told reporters. "I'd love to play him, but I'm not the one who hit .228."

Some of the team's top scouts left for the Chicago Cubs while the team picked up two more former Reds in second baseman Morgan and first baseman Tony Perez, earning the team the moniker "The Wheeze Kids." Despite their age, the Phillies were now playing with five would-be Hall of Famers on the team in Carlton, Rose, Schmidt, Morgan and Perez.

Ruly Carpenter in 1981 also decided to sell the team for $30 million to Bill Giles as Dallas Green also departed for the Cubs.

The Phils finished three games behind in 1982 when they dropped two of three in a critical series with the Cardinals in September. They also made some of their most questionable trades in club history, sending Bowa and minor league prospect, Ryne Sandberg, to the Cubs for shortstop Ivan DeJesus. Sandberg would go on to be elected into the Hall of Fame.

Maybe the biggest trade in Phillies history occurred when they sent five players, including steady second baseman Manny Trillo, to the Cleveland Indians for outfielder Von Hayes. Hayes had also been touted as the next Musial or Mantle and the Phillies bit on the hype.

In 1983 they returned to their winning form, capturing first place with 90 wins but not before Owens fired manager Pat Corrales and took the dugout helm himself on July 18. Owens said he wanted to get a feel for what the team needed. What he found is that they didn't need much.

Pitcher John Denny won the Cy Young Award going 19-6. And the team won 11 straight, 14 of their last 16 rolling into the playoffs hot. They would once again face their nemesis, The Los Angeles Dodgers, who had beaten the Phillies 11 out of 12 during their regular season games. Most people viewed the statistic as evidence that the Phillies chances were hopeless. I saw it as the odds of winning being in our favor. The Phils beat the Dodgers in six, earning their fourth pennant in history and second in four seasons.

They played in what was called the "I-95" series against the Baltimore Orioles. The Phillies won the first game before losing four straight. Like every other baseball fan, I thought I knew how to be a manager. So I was irate when Owens benched the slumping Rose after the second game. Pete had gone one for eight. But the move flabbergasted me. How do you bench arguably the greatest hitter to ever play the game? One hit and Rose could spark an entire series turnaround.

The series ended on Oct. 16 before the largest crowd ever to see a Phillies game, 67,064.

After the 1984 season in which the Phils finished fourth and 15 ½ games behind the leader, the team released Rose, who returned to the Reds and broke Ty Cobb's all-time hits record. Owens himself stepped down. In an 11-year reign as general manager, he made 47 trades, not to mention the farm club he built prior. Owens would go down as the most important member of the team management in Phillies history, leading it during its most winning period that included appearances in two World Series and five National League Championship Series.

To further dilute their team, the Phillies made another awful trade, sending ace reliever Willie Hernandez to the Detroit Tigers, where he earned the Cy Young Award.

Chapter 13
Back on the Skids

In 1985, the Phillies found themselves back in a familiar spot: battling for last place. The team won 76 games ending 26 games out of first place. A frustrated Schmidt lashed out at fans in an interview with the Montreal Gazette.

"It's a mob scene," he said. "Uncontrollable."

He said he could have accomplished more in another town and that fan pressure caused him to "try too hard." During his return to Philadelphia after the story was published, Schmidt joked about it by walking on the field in dark glasses and a long black wig acting like he was trying to disguise himself from tens of thousands of fans.

Armed with three new speedsters—Juan Samuel, Jeff Stone and Hayes—the Phils were expected to steal the division. It never happened. The team lost 34 of its first 52 games.

The Phillies added 11 more wins in 1986 but finished second to the Mets 21 ½ games behind. The foundation of their championship team began to break apart. Maddox retired while Carlton, in one of the saddest days in Philadelphia baseball history, was let go by the team. Like Phillies pitching ace Grover Alexander 70 years earlier, "Lefty" hung on with Chicago, Cleveland and finally with Minnesota winning 11 games in all.

His record of 329 wins stands second only to Warren Spahn among lefthanders in baseball history. He was second to Ryan in strikeouts and allowing the least number of walks. He spent

15 seasons with the Phillies winning 20 games in five of them and collecting four Cy Young Awards.

He had won more games than any other Phillie in history, eclipsing the greats, Roberts and Alexander.

On a positive note in the season, Schmidt picked up his third league MVP award, hitting .290 with 37 home runs and earning his 10th Gold Glove.

In 1987, I moved to Allentown to become a reporter for the newspaper, The Morning Call. What was great about living in Allentown was that I gained a chance to fulfill my wish of watching a Phillies farm club play in nearby Reading.

The Phillies Double-A team played in the old textile town and the small intimate park reminded me of Connie Mack Stadium. The hope of all Reading fans was to get to watch a player who would ultimately make his impact for the Phillies in the major leagues. Schmidt played in Reading before being called up, though he only batted .211.

The Call's science writer at the time was Rosa Salter, who was a great Phillies and Reading fan. Rosa gave us an early scouting report. The Reading Phillies had a hot infielder name Kim Batiste who showed a lot of promise. Little did we know the historical impact that he would make on our Phillies.

In Allentown, I almost got my chance to meet my boyhood idol, Taylor. He was the Phillies first base coach and I talked our sports reporter, Don Bostrom, into getting me a media pass for the locker room. But the week that I planned to go, the Phillies released Taylor, my boyhood dream dashed again.

The Phillies again played less than their expectations in 1987, finishing fourth with 80 wins and 82 losses. On April 18th, Schmidt became the 14th player in major league history to hit 500 home runs. But he was clearly unhappy with the Phillies and told reporters as much.

"We've gone from being the best of everything...to what I consider rock bottom...The minor league system is depleted...The field is the worst in the league. The dugouts are filthy. The clubhouse is dirty. The pride factor is not what it used to be," he said.

Relief pitcher Steve Bedrosian won the Cy Young Award

with 40 saves as the Phils switched managers mid-stream firing John Felske and hiring Lee Elia from the Cubs. That didn't last long. Elia's team lost their first 11 games in 1988 and managed to win only 65 for the year, finishing in the basement yet again. It was the worst Phillies summer since 1972 and Elia was fired with nine games left in the season. The only bright spot is that the Phillies made an upper level management change in hiring Lee Thomas from the Cardinals organization as its general manager.

Schmidt retired on May 29, 1989 when he was hitting a paltry .206. The man who brought cool to the Phillies uniform broke down and cried. His number "20" was retired even before the season was over. He played 16 seasons, 2,404 games and held the club record for hits (2,234), at bats (8,352), and extra base hits (1,015). He scored more runs, drove in more runs and collected more total bases than any other Phillie in team history.

His final 548 home runs placed him seventh on the all-time baseball list and was more than double the 249 hit by Del Ennis, the previous Phillies leader.

As Schmidt's exit signaled out with the old, Thomas' acquisition of a portly outfielder-first baseman from San Diego named John Kruk signaled in the new. The round West Virginia native with the cherub face and self-deprecating humor could swing a bat. He hit .300 in his first two seasons with San Diego, lucky to have roomed with hit machine and future Hall of Famer Tony Gwynn. Gwynn taught him how to study pitchers on film.

Dad and I attended a Father's Day game against the Mets and my buddy Tom Lowry took a picture of dad and I sitting together in the bleachers. It was the last game we would ever attend together. How I cherish that picture. It was a pretty awesome game too. Tom and I were hung over from carousing at the Investigative Reporters and Editors convention in town the night before. Yet we had to hang in the bleachers being sucked dry by the sun until the ninth inning because of the see-saw nature of the game, which ended with a Von Hayes walk off home run.

What may have been more important on that day was what happened after the game. The Phillies traded Samuel, who never did live up to his expectations, to the New York Mets for a pesky platoon outfielder by the name of Lenny Dysktra, a player who was described as having his mental VCR always on fast forward.

When told that the Mets had made a trade, Dykstra reportedly replied: "Who'd we get?"

The Phillies lost 32 of 44 games by midseason and was buried in the basement as Thomas fired the farm director.

A year later in 1990, we once again saw seeds of promise in our Phillies thanks to Dykstra. The center fielder and leadoff man with the wad of tobacco wedged firmly in his cheek was nicknamed the "Dude" for his hip surfer talk. He hit .325, fourth in the National League. Marching into June, he was batting .407 with a 23-game hitting streak. Dykstra was taking his place along Ashburn and Sliding Billy Hamilton as another classic Phillies leadoff hitter.

Kruk added another .291 season and a young granite-jawed catcher named Darren Daulton emerged as the leader on a team that improved 10 games over the previous year.

In 1991, the team finished third with 78 wins and 84 losses. The roster was hampered by injuries with 14 players spending some time on the disabled list during the season. The biggest headline came due to an injury off the field. Dykstra and Daulton crashed in a car leaving Kruk's bachelor party. Dykstra was charged with drunken driving of the Mercedes and broke his collarbone.

He injured himself again later in the year while running into the center field wall chasing a fly ball in Cincinnati. Dysktra had other off-field woes. He was put on one-year probation by baseball commissioner Fay Vincent for losing $78,000 in poker bets in Mississippi.

With the team struggling, Thomas hired Jim Fregosi as the manager. Unlike most Phillies managers, Fregosi had been a star baseball player having made the All-Star team six times as a premier shortstop. The Phils finished third for the season but made a nifty pickup in acquiring Mitch Williams, a relief pitcher nicknamed "The Wild Thing." Williams had been described by one of his previous employers as having a pitching style as that of a "man with his hair on fire."

In 1992, I switched teams too, taking a reporter job at The Orlando Sentinel in Florida and living for the first time out of range of the Phillies television and radio broadcasts. But the move gave me the chance to live yet another Phillies fantasy, attending Spring Training.

The crack of a bat in spring to me has always been as beautiful as the sweet sound of a chirping robin. Since 1947, the Phillies played their games at Jack Russell Stadium in Clearwater, about an hour and a half southwest of Orlando.

I was stunned at how easy it was to get tickets to the game. I just called and reserved four right behind home plate. My buddy George Post and his brother, Tom, flew down from Philadelphia and we parked ourselves behind the netting behind home plate to watch the game. That's when I heard the voice.

I turned around to see the broadcast team of Harry Kalas and Richie Ashburn sitting right behind us. I quickly hurried to buy a Phillies baseball and waited for a lull in the action to approach Ashburn, who was more than happy to sign the ball for me.

"Who do you want me to make it out to?" he asked.

"Sign it to Fred," I said, referring to dad.

We talked about some mutual pals in the newspaper business and I returned to my seat. Unfortunately, dad was in a Philadelphia nursing home by this time suffering from the onset of Alzheimer's disease. I knew he was gone when I visited him one time and found the black nurses on the floor huddled around him in his chair watching Soul Train.

When I finally did present him with the ball, I explained that I had met his favorite Phillie, Richie Ashburn, and that he had signed the ball to him.

"Oh yeah?" Dad said blankly. We had lost him but I was forever grateful to him for making me a Phillies fan.

The team sucked again. They ranked 17th in salaries among the 28 teams and played like it. They fell into the Eastern Division cellar yet again with a 70-92 record. Unbeknownst to us, they made a huge acquisition in pitching signing up an unheralded righthander named Curt Schilling from the Houston Astros.

To my joy, 1992 was also the year the team returned to wearing their old uniforms. Their hats had the script P that I wore as a child and their jerseys again contained the Phillies scrawled in italics across the chest. And then there were the red pinstripes.

My future wife, Annie, must've thought that the team name that year was "Fucking Phillies" because every day I would pick up the paper and read the sports box score muttering to myself: "Fucking Phillies." That same year, I got a chance to see the Phillies play in one of baseball's meccas, Chicago's Wrigley Field.

The Phils dropped a close one in an afternoon game. After the game, Annie and I went to the Cubs hangout, The Billy Goat Tavern. The bar was famous for the Saturday Night Live skit anchored by John Belushi, who played the Greek owner shouting "cheeseburger, cheeseburger, cheeseburger."

Annie had begged me not to walk into the bar wearing my Phillies hat, but I refused. Oddly enough, when we walked into the sea of Cubs fans, I noticed another guy with a Phillies hat all the way across the bar. He eventually came over to say hi and it was the former editorial page editor I worked with in Allentown, Randall Murray. Small Phillies world.

The team had fallen into playing like the Phillies of old too. After 10 consecutive seasons of playing .500 or better starting since 1975, the team had one winning season from 1985 through 1992. They were the only team with a losing record at the All-Star break every year from 1984 to 1992. The bullpen ranked 24th out of 26 teams, tied for second in blown saves and fourth in most relief losses with 28.

But then, as if blindsided by a bus, something magical happened.

Chapter 14
Pennant Number Five

No other baseball team could have been more perfectly matched for a city than the 1993 Phillies and Philadelphia.

If Tug McGraw was the character of the 1980s team, the team fielded 13 years later had a half dozen Tug McGraws on it. Several of them had beer bellies, giving them the look of a slow-pitch softball team. Others were ripped with muscles, spitting chewing tobacco. Yet others were just considered downright crazy.

Unlike the championship Phillies, who were groomed through the team farm system, Thomas had put his squad together by claiming refugees that other teams didn't want. He had acquired 21 of 25 players in 64 moves. Daulton described the team best when he called them: "gypsies, tramps and thieves."

The team had a surprisingly good Spring Training, going 16-10. It started the season at 3-0, its best start since 1970. The clubhouse was loose with shaving cream pies flying regularly around sections called Macho Row or the Ghetto.

Daulton became the team enforcer who would prop you up against your locker if you weren't playing to your potential while the sausage-thick Pete "Inky" Incaviglia took the spot on the field and in the batting order that Greg Luzinski once had.

"If John Kruk, Darren Daulton and Pete Incaviglia were all in the same grade school class, they wouldn't be allowed to sit together," wrote George King of the Trenton Times.

64

The clubhouse beermeister held two kegs that were changed every three games.

"If crazy is running out ground balls, playing hard and getting your uniform dirty, then, yeah they're crazy," Fregosi told the press of his squad.

The team faced the largest opening crowd ever at 61,000. The turning point for the team came in an early season game on April 26 when the San Francisco Giants jumped to an 8-0 laughable lead. The Phils came roaring back to win it, 9-8, putting the club 10 games over .500 for the first time in seven years. They also beat the Cubs 11-10 in the same month.

The Phillies finished the month 17-5, the most successful April in club history. They occupied first place for the first time on May 1 since the dreaded 1964 team as the organization had to hire more ticket sales people to handle the deluge.

They sailed to an 11 ½ game lead by mid-June but fell into a tailspin losing 14 of 20 games watching their lead drop to three. In September, Montreal got hot winning 17 of 20 and reducing the Phillies lead to four games, once again resurrecting the ghosts of 1964.

"Sure, we heard about 1964," outfielder Milt Thompson told reporters. "But most of the guys weren't even born in 1964."

One of the heroes on the team was right-fielder Jim Eisenreich. Eisenreich suffered from Turret's Syndrome, which caused him to have nervous ticks. But the man could hit, batting at least .300 in each of his four seasons with the Phillies.

Our Reading prospect, Kim Batiste, was on the team, hitting .282 with five homers, half of his career total. But he was treasured for his infield defense, often serving as a substitute late in the game.

The team gained national attention for its scruffy look. Kruk, in particular, served as the poster boy for the team, often caking his batting helmet with pine tar.

"Honest, we're really not bad people," Kruk told one journalist. "But you wouldn't want us in your home."

The classic Kruk story came in Spring Training when a woman scolded him for being an athlete and smoking. "I ain't no athlete, lady" Kruk was said to have replied. "I'm a ballplayer."

One sports writer described Kruk as Oscar Madison, Pig Pen and Oscar the Grouch rolled into one. In a 2006 book about the team entitled "Beards, Bellies and Biceps," the Phillie Phanatic Dave Raymond said Kruk's locker looked more like a trailer park. Mitch Williams often joked that Kruk signed with the team for $500 and a gift certificate to Waffle House.

Kruk called the team "throwbacks."

"We're a throwback all right," Kruk said. "Thrown back by other organizations."

But nobody argued that Kruk could hit. For the season, he hit .316 with 14 homers and 85 runs batted in. Dysktra credited Fregosi with being able to harness the team's youthful energy.

"Some managers you just play for," Dykstra said to the media. "Some you really want to fucking win for."

And win they did. The team didn't have the raw talent of the 1980 championship team, but was more like a story that resembled "Rocky," the 1976 boxing movie made in Philadelphia. They fought. They won a 20-inning game against the Dodgers. They were 8-2 in extra inning games, 15-6 in one run games and 10 and 8 in two run games.

"I can't imagine that any other city ever had a team better matched to it," Mayor Ed Rendell told the press. "Those '93 Phillies had to be one of the all-time blue-collar squads."

The fans quickly fell in love with them too. The team crested over the 3 million attendance mark for the season, recording 16 dates with more than 50,000 fans and 20 consecutive games when attendance reached 40,000.

"In Philly," Kruk told sports writers. "The fans make you concentrate."

The Phillies won 97 games, the most since their championship season, and tied a major league mark for staying in first place for all but one day of the season. They were only the second team of the century to go from last to first in back-to-back seasons.

The National League Championship Series was against the defending pennant champion Atlanta Braves, who were dubbed "America's Team" because of their national cable contract with

Turner Broadcasting, which owned the team. Atlanta had won 104 games, seven more than the Phils and were heavy favorites having played in two previous World Series.

The teams had split their regular season games, 6-6, yet the Phillies led the Braves by 10 points in what was considered the most important statistic in baseball: getting runners on base. The Phils had scored 877 runs, the most of any team in 40 years.

The Atlanta media was having fun with the Phillies' image, described by one writer as "a roving gang of bikers." The Atlanta Journal Constitution warned readers to "hide their women and children" when the Phillies arrived. If Atlanta was "America's Team," the Phillies were "America's Most Wanted" team.

"America's Team Against Wild-eyed, Tobacco spittin', Gut bustin' Phillies," a Journal headline proclaimed.

The Phils threw the first punch of the series, knocking Atlanta down 4-3 behind the exceptional pitching of Schilling who struck out the first five Braves batters. Schilling had won 16 games in the regular season, losing seven and making him the most dominant pitcher on the Phillies squad since Carlton.

A visible pattern developed. Whenever the Phillies contended for the pennant, they did so on the backs of a strong starting pitchers such as Alexander, Roberts, Carlton and now Schilling.

The game one win didn't come easy. Batiste, put in defensively late in the game at third, committed a throwing error in the 9th that helped the Braves score the tying run. But he redeemed himself in the 10th, knocking in the game-winning run and was hoisted off the field on the shoulders of his teammates.

Atlanta won game two by a football score, 14-3. The Phillies also lost the third game, 9-4, when Sentinel columnist Brian Schmitz called the series over. The Atlanta bats were too dominant against flawed Phillies pitching, he said.

"And now a moment of silence for the Philadelphia Phillies pitching staff," Schmitz wrote. "The Phillies are a memory and a bad one at that."

Schmitz resorted to the hackneyed characterization of the scruffy Phils.

"You think they could shave and use a little mousse and look respectable at their own wake," he said.

The column enraged me and I whipped out my typewriter to file a response. Criticizing another reporter was like a doctor testifying against another doctor, it rarely happened. But I warned Schmitz not to knock the Phillies out. After all, they had won 97 games and stayed on top of the division all year.

Incaviglia may have put it best when he was quoted as saying: "This ain't no fucking beauty show, it's baseball."

I finished the letter in true Phillie fan fashion.

"Don't hit your ass falling off the bandwagon," I wrote.

The Phils carried a 2-1 lead into the 9th inning of game four when Williams came into pitch and double-dribbled a bunt that resulted in the Braves having two men on with nobody out. The cameras zoomed in on Schilling with a towel over his head, unable to watch. Williams was able to get out of the jam, despite throwing a grounder wide of third base that Batiste had to miraculously stab.

Game 5 resembled its predecessor with the Phillies marching into the ninth inning with a 3-0 lead. Batiste again bobbled a grounder, creating a two-man on nobody out situation. The Braves tied the game in the bottom of the ninth, sending it into extra innings.

But Dykstra hit a blast in the 10th to give the Phillies the win and glared at Braves owner, Ted Turner and Turner's girlfriend, Jane Fonda, as he rounded first base. The Phils were one game from the pennant.

I decided to watch the sixth game of the series in my own house. I didn't like watching games in bars because of the crowd noise and distractions. And watching at home allowed me to jump and shout and throw things. But with the Phillies up 2-1 heading into the bottom of the fifth, I got a frantic call from Chris O'Keefe.

O'Keefe was a Philly native whose family owned an Irish restaurant in Tavares called O'Keefe's Tavern On The Lake. The pub was probably the finest Irish bar I was ever in, including ale houses in Ireland. Chris was a Phillies die-hard, his father having grown up in the city.

"You've got to help me man," he said into the phone. "I'm all by myself with six of the biggest, ugliest Braves fans you'd ever want to see."

I drove down to the bar with my Phillies hat on and sure enough, along the side row of the bar were six menacing Braves fans who looked like wrestlers but worked on the county fire department. What I hadn't realized living in Florida was that before the state got its own teams in Tampa and Miami, most Florida residents rooted for the Braves, who were then the closest team.

The Phils went up 6-1 by the bottom of the sixth and O'Keefe and I were rubbing it in, hooting and hollering at the stoic Braves supporters. The Braves bounced back, closing the gap to 6-3 and we weren't talking so much trash. Williams came in the ninth again and shut down the Braves 1-2-3, striking out pinch hitter Bill Pecot at 11:17 p.m. as the Phillies won their fifth pennant in its 110 year history to date and Williams leaped off the mound pumping his fist into the air.

Fully drunk at 2 a.m. when the tavern closed, I drove home with my sun roof open and my head poking out, beeping my horn and shouting: "The Phillies Won the Pennant! The Phillies Won the Pennant!" All I could think about the next day was some senior citizen waking up the next morning and asking her husband: "Harold, what's a Phillie?"

Washington Post baseball writer Tom Boswell, considered one of the nation's premier authorities on the game, gave his assessment of the Phillies.

"The Phillies don't play baseball right," Boswell wrote. "They are an aesthetic abomination. They play anti-baseball and revel in it. In fact, they might not even know what the rules are. Any normal team rolls over and dies after such an embarrassment in Games 2 and 3. And just when you think they'll quit, they spit in your eye."

The Phillies would have to face the defending World Champion Toronto Blue Jays in the World Series. They received the same respect from the Toronto press as they did in

Atlanta.

"They chew, they spit, they cuss and they belch," Toronto Star columnist Rosie Dimanno wrote. "They are a species that could be found tippling brewskies in a Legion hall, a slo-pitch team sponsored by Billy Bob's hardware perhaps, except this particular group of hardy 'n' lardy sportsmen have made it to the World Series."

Toronto was the heavy favorites having strung together 11 straight winning seasons, winning over 1,000 games and making the playoffs four out of the five previous years. But going to the championship, Tug McGraw told reporters, made all teams even.

"I'll tell you what October is all about," McGraw said. "There isn't a player on the field who isn't running on fumes. Your tanks are empty and you're trying to see who can crawl across the finish line first."

Toronto won the first game at home 8-5 but the Phils bounced back in Game 2, 6-4. With the split, they were heading back to Philadelphia to play three games, giving the Phillies the advantage.

"There is no city like Philadelphia when it comes to sports," wrote Boston Globe writer Michael Madden. "Cruel. Hard. Tough. Mean."

Toronto won in a laugher, 10-3, and the Phillies stranded nine runners, bringing their three game total to 29. They were getting their men on base, but not knocking them home. They weren't playing Phillies baseball.

Game 4 was a slugfest with Toronto collecting six runs in the eighth inning to win 15-14. Williams was the loser, giving up the three final runs on three hits and a walk. Toronto had scored an amazing 25 runs in two games, more than their whole World Series total the previous year.

The Phillies fans were getting restless. A sign hung from the rafters in Game 5 proclaiming: "Will pitch middle relief for food." But Schilling pitched a gem, scattering five hits and three walks in a complete game as the Phils won 2-0.

I had tickets for the Orlando Magic basketball game the night of the sixth game of the World Series and I was hoping the Magic game would end early enough for me to get home and catch the Phillies. As I was leaving the arena, I spotted Jimmy Leusner, a colleague who grew up in South Jersey, a Phillies haven. Leusner had been listening to the game on the radio and gave me the bad news. The Phils were down 5-1 after six.

By the time I got home, the Phillies rally had started. They scored five runs in the top of the seventh, including a three-run homer by Dykstra, to take a 6-5 lead. I believed a Phils win would give them enough momentum to win the final game.

Fregosi brought in Williams to pitch the bottom of the ninth, a decision that will be forever second-guessed in Phillies history. Williams hadn't pitched well in the series but he had a Phillies record 43 saves for the season. Every fan acts like the manager in such situations and though I knew Williams was sagging, I believed in the loyal saying that you have to stick with the dogs that "brung 'ya."

Williams walked the leadoff batter, consummate base stealer Rickey Henderson. The next batter flied out to left before Paul Molitor hit a single. Up to the plate stepped Joe Carter, a player the Phillies ironically tried to acquire in the off season.

The count went to two balls and two strikes when Carter got a piece of the ball and slammed it into left field for only the second walk-off home run to win a World Series in league history. Dykstra described to sports writers the feeling of watching the ball leaving the field.

"I didn't want to watch it," he said. "I really thought this was meant to be our year. We battled and battled and battled."

Williams received death threats and vandals egged his house. The joke around town was that the eggs were thrown by Mitch himself trying to hit his neighbor's house. Again, McGraw put it in perspective to the media.

"The difference between Mitch and me in that situation is a half-inch," he said. "Willie Wilson missed my pitch by a half-inch. Carter got Mitch's pitch by a half-inch."

I was back at Spring Training in Clearwater the following year sitting next to a man who kept taking pictures of the grass in left field. I finally asked him what he was doing.

"I'm from upper Canada," he said. "We don't see grass until August."

From that point on, we began buying each other beers, me saluting his team's World Series victory and him saluting the Phillies effort. The game ended in the ninth when the Phillies scored a walk-off run with a thrilling close play at the plate, an omen we hoped meant good things for 1994. But it wasn't meant to be.

The Phils finished fourth, 20 ½ games out of first place. Stars like Dysktra, Daulton and Kruk, who was diagnosed with testicular cancer, missed huge chunks of the season. But it was the year Carlton was inducted into the Hall of Fame and the year I got to meet McGraw.

I was covering the World Cup soccer games in Orlando when they threw a party for the Ireland team at Sea World. I was standing around sipping a beer when I turned and saw him.

"Tug!" I shouted, startling him. "Willie Wilson, 1980."

McGraw was polite and tried to calm my excitement. He had been living near Tampa working as a representative for retired baseball players. Later in the night, I sat on the back porch of the place drinking beers and talking with him about watching the soccer games. I ended up writing a story about how a World Series pitcher views World Cup soccer. McGraw said he was having trouble picking up the fouls.

A players strike shortened the season and stretched into 1995 when the Phillies finished in a tie for second but still 21 games behind the leader. The highlight of the season occurred off the field on July 30 when Ashburn and Schmidt were inducted into the Hall of Fame together.

Ashburn had been boxed out of the institution since he retired in 1962. His squabbles with the sports writers had cost him. But 33 years later, the veterans committee welcomed him into the club.

Phillies fans climbed on 171 buses to Cooperstown, creating a sea of red at the induction ceremony. Schmidt, a first-ballot selection with the most points total to date, settled his differences with the fans in his induction speech.

"I know you cared and for that I thank you," he said.

Schmidt thanked three players for helping his career: Boone, Rose and oddly enough, Dick Allen. The day went down as one of the greatest in Phillies sports history.

Chapter 15
Another New Century

As it had through most of the 1900s, the Phillies limped into the new century.

In 1997, the team finished fifth, 33 games out of first place. One bright spot was the play of their new third baseman, Scott Rolen. The team thought they had found their new Mike Schmidt in Rolen, who won the Rookie of the Year award hitting .282 with 21 home runs and 92 runs batted in. The team signed Rolen to a four-year $10 million contract.

In a reminder of the Curt Flood saga, though, the team had also drafted J.D. Drew, an outfielder who had also garnered comparisons to Musial and Mantle. Drew wanted an $11 million contract, but the Phils were only willing to offer him the standard $2 million rookie package. As a result, he returned to the minors for a year before signing with the St. Louis Cardinals and Philadelphia was jilted yet again.

Schilling, a stalwart remnant from the 1993 pennant team, continued his winning ways, going 17-11. But the franchise also experienced heartbreak when Richie Ashburn died in his sleep in a New York hotel.

The team got better in 1998 when it won seven games over the previous year and finished third under manager Terry Francona. A new general manager, Ed Wade, took over for Thomas and four of the team's eight position players were new as the Phillies were in flux. They picked up stars in Bobby Abreu and Doug Glanville while Schilling became only the fifth player in major league history to record back to back 300 strikeout seasons.

In 1999, they ended the 20th century with a result they were accustomed to: losing. Their record of 77-85 meant that it was the 64th losing season of the century. Catcher Mike Lieberthal and Abreau hit over .300 while the team recorded 161 home runs, the most of the Phillies' century and Schilling went 15-6, pitching in the All-Star game.

I took a job as the City Hall reporter at The Baltimore Sun and for the first time in my life had more closely followed another team besides the Phillies, The Baltimore Orioles. I would sneak out of work on opening day to get a $9 bleacher seat in Camden Yards, the retro park that had been touted as the national example for new baseball stadiums.

It had reminded me of Connie Mack Stadium with its red brick walls and grass field. Former Orioles slugger Boog Powell sold barbecue sandwiches behind right field, the gray smoke floating over the stadium filled with a charcoal scent. And my only wish was that dad could see it. I watched Orioles slugging first baseman Eddie Murray hit his 500th home run.

It was at Camden Yards where I finally met my boyhood idol, Tony Taylor. He was the infield coach for the Florida Marlins, who were playing a three game series. I talked the sports department into giving me a locker room pass and went down into the stadium. I opened the locker room door and there he was. I knew it was him from my baseball card collection, though he was obviously much older.

"I'm looking for Tony Taylor," I said.

"Tony Taylor?" he said in his stilted Cuban accent. "He no here. He died. He an old man."

I chuckled.

"Nah, he's not," I said. "He's the greatest Phillies second baseman to ever play the game."

We shook hands and smiled as if we were old friends. He talked about his love for playing at Camden Yards, which he said reminded him of Connie Mack stadium. He was living in Florida and hoping to stay with the Marlins two more years in order to get full retirement benefits.

He was traveling the next day to have lunch with Bunning,

now a Kentucky Republican U.S. senator. It was Taylor who had saved Bunning's perfect game by stabbing a shot up the middle. He knocked the ball down and threw out the Mets' slow moving pitcher, Jesse Gonder.

We had someone snap our picture, my dream come true.

The 2000 season for the Phillies was their worst finish since 1972, winning 65 games and finishing last in their division. The record meant that they had 14 losing seasons out of their last 15. Mercifully, Schilling was dealt to the Arizona Diamondbacks, where he finally won his World Series ring a year later.

In 2001, the team injected some much needed excitement when it hired Larry Bowa as its manager. The fiery former shortstop who resurrected memories of the team's only championship immediately put the Phillies into overdrive. They won 86 games and finished in second place, battling Atlanta for the division lead til the last week of the season when they finished two games behind. Until that year, the team hadn't come within 20 games of the division leader.

Bowa won Manager of the Year honors as the team posted its best record since the 1993 pennant. Abreau became the first Phillie ever to hit 30 home runs and steal 30 bases.

But in a reminder of Richie Allen, Rolen expressed his displeasure with the Phillies. He clashed with Bowa and questioned the team management's commitment to winning. He had a subpar Spring Training, which caused fans to get on him. And he turned down a $140 million package offered by the team. In July of 2002, he got his wish and was dealt to the first-place Cardinals.

The Phillies dug a hole for themselves in April that they never got out of, going 9-18. The team finished third, 21 ½ games out with an 80-81 record.

The next year was the last for the 32-year-old Veterans Stadium. Like former Phillies parks, it had its share of mishaps. One year during an Army-Navy game, a front row railing broke sending military fans crashing 30 yards below. And in the stadium's waning years, The Baltimore Ravens refused to play an exhibition game because the turf was in such a deplorable condition.

The Phils continued to hang in the middle of the division pack. In December, the team had signed free agent slugger Jim Thome from the Cleveland Indians to the most lucrative contract in team history. Thome would receive $85 million over six years with a $10 million signing bonus. Riding in a limousine near where the team's ballpark was being built, Thome came across a pack of electricians holding up signs urging him to join. He stopped the car and greeted them.

He was lobbied by others, such as Rose, Thome's boyhood idol who assured him what a great sports town Philly was to play in. Thome became a fan favorite, always making curtain calls after hitting home runs, signing autographs and talking with the media.

In his first year, he hit 47 home runs, one shy of Schmidt's record, and drove in 131 runs. Bowa, on the other hand, began feuding with players, questioning their intensity in hopes of spurring them to the top like a jockey whipping his horse in the final lengths. It almost worked. The Phillies had a lock on the wild-card playoff spot late in the season until they were swept in a series by the Marlins, who went on to win the World Championship with two former Phillies, Eisenreich and Daulton.

But the Phillies were showing promise again. Four pitchers won at least 14 games. Lieberthal hit .313 and Abreau had his regular solid season batting .300 and driving in 101 runs.

In 2004, the team opened Citizens Bank Park, which looked much like Baltimore's stadium with its red-brick motif, grass field and a center field that had the city skyline as its backdrop. Attendance surged to over 3 million. Yet the Phils finished 10 games behind Atlanta, not even close in the wild-card race.

It was also the year the team lost Tug McGraw. The Phillies pitching jester developed brain cancer and died on Jan. 5. One of my last memories of him was seeing him on television at the Phillies St. Patrick's Day Spring Training game when the team wore green, including a green hat with the white Phillies "P."

Bowa left the team with a few games remaining in the season, his confrontational style having alienated players.

Meanwhile, former Phillies manager Terry Francona coached the Red Sox to winning the World Series.

By 2005, the team had the highest payroll in baseball at $95 million. Thome was sidelined with an elbow injury that led to the emergence of power-hitting rookie first baseman, Ryan Howard. At 6-feet-4 and 255 lbs., Howard was the reincarnation of Richie Allen, without the controversy. In his first half season, he hit 22 home runs and batted .288, winning Rookie of the Year honors much like Allen had done.

But the team finished one game out of the playoffs, despite being tied for the eastern division lead with 16 games left.

Before 2006, Thome was traded to the White Sox as the Phillies put their stock in Howard and it almost paid off. The youth hit a new Phillies record 58 home runs and won the league's Most Valuable Player award. The team traded Abreau to the already talent stocked New York Yankees. Fans again began questioning the Phillies management's commitment to winning as the payroll dropped to $88 million, 12th in the league.

It was when I met Bunning too. I worked as a reporter in the Senate Press Gallery of the Capitol as the Washington correspondent for a paper in Baton Rouge, La. I stepped on the Senate subway one day and there he was sitting alone.

"Father's Day, 1964," I said. A broad smile swept across his face.

"Good memory," he said.

"My father never forgot that day," I said. "I grew up in the Kensington section of the city."

"That's a good place to leave," Bunning said.

"You didn't like Philadelphia?" I asked.

"They were the best six years of my life," he said.

I told him that I had a collection of balls with stamped autographs of Phillies Hall of Famers that Burger King had put out one season. My sister collected them for me, Mike Schmidt, Richie Ashburn, Robin Roberts and Steve Carlton.

"I wonder why I wasn't included in that?" he said.

That's when I threw the wild pitch.

"Because you were never elected to the Hall of Fame," I

said.

Major error. Bunning was inducted in 1996, the first pitcher since Cy Young himself to win 100 games and strike out 1,000 batters in both leagues. Bunning was kind and didn't correct me as we stepped off the subway and proceeded to our duties.

I later traded him one of his baseball cards if he would sign a Phillies ball, which he graciously did and I mistakenly slid it into my pocket, where the ink smudged off. My dad's Ashburn ball also got smudged because I kept it in a plastic bag. I was collecting the best smudged Phillies Hall of Fame balls that anyone could want.

Despite being tied with the Dodgers for the wild-card playoff berth with six games left in the season, the 2006 team finished runner-up by 3 games to the Dodgers after losing two out of three in the final week to the lowly Washington Nationals. I couldn't help to think that the Phillies would've had an all-star team if they could've managed to retain Thome, Abreau, Drew, Rolen and added Howard.

As the season ended, I got panicked e-mail from O'Keefe expressing his chagrin.

"They disappointed us again!!!" he said.

The Phillies marched into the 2007 with unusual bravado. Hotshot shortstop Jimmy Rollins predicted before the season started that the Phils would be the team to beat in the Eastern Division.

That didn't sit too well with the New York Mets, who won the division a year earlier, and the Atlanta Braves, the Phillies old nemesis who had been knocking on the playoff door in 2006.

And in the first half of the season, Rollins prediction proved right: everybody was beating the Phillies. The team started off with 4 wins and 11 losses, the worst start in the major leagues.

Within striking distance 5 games out of first place, the Phillies rolled into a critical four-game weekend series with the Mets a week before the All-Star game break. The Mets won three out of four, keeping the Phillies at a safe distance.

The next month, the Phillies achieved the dubious dishonor

of having lost their 10,000 game of all time, giving them more losses than any other franchise in American sports history.

At the time of the infamous loss, the Phillies had even lost 570 more games than the hapless Chicago Cubs. The Braves, who were also one of the oldest teams in the league, were in second place, 333 losses behind the Phillies.

Phillies representatives tried to put their best face on it. The Phillies were one of the oldest organizations in the league starting in 1883, they explained. And nobody remembers that the team had won close to 9,000 games.

The Phillies' 10,000 loss came on Sunday, July 15 to the St. Louis Cardinals, ironically the team that won the 1964 pennant. The 10-2 loss that numbered 10,000 came in typical Phillies fashion—bad starting pitching, crippled relief work and silent bats.

Phillies fans relished the honor. A packed crowd of 45,000 held up signs such as: "10,000 N Proud." Others had hoped to stave off the embarrassment with signs such as: "10,000 Is Not in the Cards."

Just before the big day, I was staying at a dairy farm in Lancaster County, Pa. big Phillies fan territory—and happened to be wearing my Phillies jersey. A milk farmer, who had been down to the game the night before and saw the team lose in a 12-8 slugfest to Detroit, happened to comment on my shirt.

"You know heartache too," he said.

After the All-Star break, the Phillies rolled like a wagon downhill, gaining momentum and winning more games than they lost each month. The team came from behind to win 48 times, the most of any other team in baseball.

Their play provided one of the most stunning season finishes in recent memory. The Mets were in first place with a 7 game lead over the Phillies on Sept. 12.

But the New Yorkers suddenly collapsed, losing 12 of their last 16 games. Meanwhile the Phillies became torrid, winning 13 of their last 17. I attended one game in Washington where the Phillies defeated the Nationals 6-3 and Howard knocked out one of his league leading 47 home runs.

The following week the Phillies were playing their last three games at home facing the Nationals. They went into the weekend tied with the Mets. If the Phillies could win three and the Mets lose one, they would fulfill Rollins prediction and capture the eastern division.

Both the Phillies and the Mets ended up losing one of the weekend games and were tied going into the last day of the season on Sunday. If both teams won they would have to play a one game playoff—similar to 1950.

Fans had once again caught Phillies fever and were shown on national television—over 45,000 strong—waving short white towels handed out before the game. As the Phillies were batting in the first inning of the final game, the crowd roared when the score of the Mets game from the first inning was posted: Florida Marlins 7, New York Mets 1.

The Phillies won their final game, 6-1, while the Mets ended with an 8-1 loss, giving the Phils the eastern division banner. It was a stunning end to a wild season and left the Mets with the biggest collapse in baseball history, except of course for the 1964 Phillies.

Jimmy Rollins backed up his boasting, hitting .296. And he became only the fourth player in major league history to hit more than 20 doubles, triples and home runs while having 20 steals. The numbers made him the league Most Valuable Player, the second consecutive for the Phillies.

Howard continued to dominate the league in hitting, leading the team with 136 runs batted in.

But again, the Phillies team was lopsided. It placed fifth in hitting, including ranking second in home runs. It led the league in what baseball analysts say is the most important statistic: runs. The Phillies punched home almost 900 runners.

In true Phillies fashion, team pitching was fourth from the bottom. They may have located their ace in the young Cole Hamels, who went 15-5 for the season, but the team ended up relying on a franchise record 28 pitchers due to injuries and a shaky bullpen.

The Phillies faced the Colorado Rockies in the playoffs and were quickly tossed aside, losing three straight to the team that were league leaders in batting. The young Phillies pitchers were rocked and rattled while the bats at the top of the order, that included Rollins and Howard, failed to come through.

Though it was another disappointing finish, Phillies fans were excited that the team made it to the playoffs. Fans were pumped up with the drama of that final week of the season. And true to form the dreaded New York Yankees made it to their 13th consecutive playoff while Schilling, Drew and Francona led Boston to its second World Series in four years.

I infected my own Phillies fan, my 5-year-old son Liam, that summer. He was attracted to my bright red Phillies hat with the white italic P and wanted one of his own. He would wake up each morning and ask whether the Phillies won and whether they were playing that day.

I was stymied at how I would find a Phillies hat for a little boy in Washington Nationals territory, but there it was hanging on a rack all by itself in a Union Station shop. And I placed it on his head as if crowning him as he beamed a smile, joyous over his "Phillie hat."

Chapter 16
Hope Over Experience

Despite the endless losses, the disappointing seasons and the heartbreaking playoff dead ends, I remained a loyal Philadelphia Phillies fan.

I wore my Phillies tee-shirt and shorts to bed in the summer and checked the box scores every day, even though I'm living in Washington Nationals country. I once asked a colleague who had been through a bitter divorce why he intended to get married again. He said it was triumph of hope over experience.

That's what being a Phillies fan means. Every Spring, despite past disappointments, when the crack of the bat signaled a new season there was hope. You dreamed that your team was going to somehow win it all and be a shining example of the city to the rest of the nation. And the fans of the more than two dozen teams around the league felt the same way even though only one team could win it all.

The Phillies headed into the 2008 season with little change in their lineup, which caused me concern. The dastardly New York Mets went out and traded for Johan Santana, a two-time American League Cy Young winner, significantly boosting their pitching firepower.

The biggest Phillies move was obtaining 31-year old relief pitcher from the Houston Astros named Brad Lidge. Lidge became the Phillies "closer," the final relief pitcher brought into games when the Phillies are leading to make sure the other team doesn't come back and win. The two most memorable Phillies closers in recent memory were Mitch Williams and

McGraw from the World Series days.

Lidge had spent his career with the Astros and I didn't think he was a good pickup. He only saved 19 games the year before and had knee surgery in the off season. He tore it again during one of his first trips to the mound in Spring Training.

And when he was in the minor leagues at the turn of the century, Lidge had a torn rotator cuff and even broke his forearm threatening to end his career.

But what he was most remembered for was two home runs he gave up. One was a three-run homer to lose a playoff game in 2005. Later in the World Series, he gave up the winning home run to end the game, evoking memories of Williams.

So here I thought we were putting our stock in a broken down reliever while our arch rivals went out a picked up a superstar.

Lidge, however, had been an All-Star in 2005, saving an impressive 42 games. And he wasn't nicknamed "Lights Out" for no reason. He shut down batters with screaming fastball and was the all-time leader in strikeouts per nine innings.

The Phillies made little change in their pitching rotation. The 24-year-old Hamels was the anchor and the Phils were looking for double-digit wins from an ace that was starting to look like his hero, Steve Carlton, and 1993 Phillies World Series ace Curt Schilling

The other pitcher they relied on was Brett Myers. Myers was as big as a football player, 6-feet-4 and 240 pounds who threw hard. Prior to 2008, Myers had been a solid pitcher for the Phillies before getting hurt in 2007 and being relegated to the bullpen.

Myers was also known most for his off-the-field antics. He was arrested in 2006 for punching his wife on a Boston street. The charges were dropped when she chose not to prosecute. He was involved in another altercation in 2007 when he went after a reporter who asked him about giving up two home runs in a game.

The third starter was Jamie Moyer, the oldest player in baseball at the time. Moyer, a lefty, had been pitching for 22 years, first bouncing around with the Cubs, Cardinal, Detroit

Tigers and Orioles before landing a steady gig with the Seattle Mariners in 1996.

His addition to the Phillies was a dream come true for him because he grew up in Sellersville, a Philadelphia suburb. He pitched for one of the city's most known colleges, St. Joseph's University, where he set the school's single season strikeout record of 90 in 1984.

One of his most memorable experiences was being among the throngs of fans at the 1980 parade for the world champion Phillies. Moyer joined over two million people who lined the streets to cheer Carlton, Rose, Schmidt, McGraw and the others riding on floats down Broad Street.

Moyer pitched his first game for the Chicago Cubs in 1986 against his boyhood idol, Steve Carlton, beating the Phillies 7-5. Moyer said later that his career could've ended after that game and he would have been satisfied.

Moyer was a consistently good pitcher. In 1997, he won 17 games losing only 5, the second highest winning percentage in the league. A year later, he won 15 games and 14 more in 1999. In 2001 and 2003, he was a 20-game winner and an All-Star.

Not only did Moyer succeed on the field, but he captured every award from the Roberto Clemente Award to the Lou Gehrig Award for his off-the-field contributions. He started a foundation for kids who experienced severe personal distress and trauma. Moyer himself had poured millions of his own money to the non-profit cause.

He joined the Phillies in 2006, when he went 5-2. It was Moyer who pitched 5 1/3 shutout innings against the Nationals to clinch the playoff spot the year before. But the question always lingered: when would this man approaching 50 start to fade?

Going into the season, it was the Mets who were talking trash this time. With the addition of Santana, players were quoted telling Rollins that they were the team to beat to win the division.

"With Johan Santana now, I have no doubt we're going to win our division," said Carlos Beltran. "So to Jimmy Rollins, we are the team to beat."

The Phillies started off solid, winning 15 games and losing 13. It was the first winning April in seven seasons and only their fourth since the 1993 World Series team and it kept them ½ game behind the league leading Florida Marlins.

Utley was on fire, hitting .360 with a league-leading 11 home runs. He helped make up for the silent bat of the team lumberjack, Howard, who was hitting a paltry .172 with only two hits in the whole month.

Hamels continued to show himself as the team ace, winning three games in the first month. His dominance was visible in May as the Phillies took first place, switching places with Florida.

Howard got back on track improving his batting average by 80 points and hitting 10 home runs. And Lidge was proving to be a more than worthy pickup, recording 12 saves when the Phillies led in the late innings.

In May, the offense started rolling scoring 60 runs in five games including a 20-5 win over the Colorado Rockies.

June was like playing two different months for the Phillies. Pitching and hitting were clicking in the first half. From May 26 to June 13, the team posted a 14-4 record and were winning by football scores.

Their run started with a 15-6 win over the Astros and ended with beating the Cardinals, 20-2. Utley and Howard became the first Phillies pair ever to have 15 home runs each by June.

But the team only won 3 games the remainder of the month, losing 11. Though Hamels pitched strong, winning three games that month, other Phillies pitchers struggled, most notably Myers. His inconsistent play relegated him to the bullpen before earning him a trip to the minor leagues to regain confidence and work on his mechanics.

Utley and Lidge were named to the All-Star team as the Phillies kept a razor thin lead over the nemesis Mets and Lidge now had 19 straight saves. Before the month was out they made a trade to acquire an unknown pitcher by the name of Joe Blanton.

In August, the team slipped falling into third place by Sept.

10, behind both the Mets and Florida. Though their opponents' leads were slight, any Phillies slide backward stirred up memories of past collapses.

My childhood buddy Georgie Post got the dream job of a lifetime as an usher at the Phillies games.

I couldn't wait to see George to hear what it was like to try to control what many people believed were the most unruly fans in the nation. And George didn't disappoint.

One of his first memorable tasks was throwing two guys out for fighting. When he got to their seats, one of the guys was drenched in beer.

"It was an accident," the other said.

"Right," George said. "You didn't throw it and he didn't wear it now get out."

My favorite story was about the couple who were discovered in the bathroom having sex. The two said they were married with five kids. No wonder, George thought.

As he led them out of the stadium, the women made one last plea before being kicked out.

"Did you ever have a fantasy?" she asked George.

"Yeah," he said. "But it didn't involve having bathroom sex in a stadium with 42,000 people."

Another memorable trip to the bathroom involved a man hiding in the stall of the women's room. George confronted him about what he was doing in there.

"I was talking to a girl," he said.

"Well," George said. "This would be a good place to do that. Now get out."

Chapter 17
See You In September

The true architect of the new and improved Phillies was general manager Pat Gillick.

He had been the general manager for four teams since 1978. All had advanced into the league championship playoffs. Two Toronto Blue Jays teams won back-to-back World Series, including the dreaded squad that beat the Phillies in 1993.

Gillick guided the Baltimore Orioles to the American championship series twice in the 1990s and took the Seattle Mariners to the mountain twice between 1999 and 2003. None of the teams that Gillick left ever made it back to the playoffs.

Having joined the Phillies two years earlier, the 71-year-old baseball whiz, who was calling the 2008 season his last, guided the Phillies to the National League East title in his second year with the team.

Moyer pitched for Gillick in Seattle and never questioned the general manager's moves.

"It just seems like there's always a reason for what he does," Moyer told The New York Times. "The guy's had success pretty much everywhere he's been, so he's doing something right."

Five seasons before Gillick arrived in Philadelphia, the team was consistently knocking on the playoff door winning 80 to 88 games a year. But they failed to reach the playoffs, coming up just shy of the 90 plus wins that were necessary.

Gillick put together this Phillies team stealthily, grabbing no name players from around the league. He went after Lidge, who ended up being a great catch with a perfect 41 saves for all 41 games he pitched for the season, making me feel bad that I doubted him.

Gillick made unpopular moves, like sending Abreau to the Yankees. But the move saved the team $20 million and opened a center field spot for a little-known player named Shane Victorino, who the Dodgers threw away from their minor league system.

Thome was also a fan favorite that Gillick dished, putting his stock in Howard. He picked up right fielder Jayson Werth, who had been plagued by injuries with the Dodgers, including a broken wrist the year before. Gillick had drafted Werth into the league when he was general manager with Baltimore.

"He's had some injuries over the past couple of years, but we think he has tremendous athleticism and we're very happy to have him in a Phillies uniform," Gillick told the press.

Werth ended up hitting 24 home runs for the Phillies during the season including three in one game with one being a grand slam. And he helped save the team in the early part of the season when stars, such as Jimmy Rollins, were hurt.

Another pickup was pinch hitter Matt Stairs, a consistent home run hitter who had bounced around the league for 20 years with no less than 11 teams. He only appeared in 16 Phillies games during the season but hit close to .300. Gillick also found Gregg Dobbs, a pinch hitter who could also play third base and who hit .300 for the team for the season. As general manager for the Mariners, Gillick drafted Dobbs into the league.

Gillick's baseball intellect was unquestioned. He graduated high school at 16 and college at 20. He was a gifted pitcher with the University of Southern California, playing on the 1958 national title team.

He spent five years in the minor leagues and in 1963 became the farm system assistant to the Houston Colt .45s, who later became the Astros.

He first started studying players when he became director of scouting for the Astros in 1974. He then served as scouting director for the New York Yankees for two seasons just before the Reggie Jackson hey days in the 70s.

(Most people don't know that Jackson grew up in Philly. I once met his father, who owned a tailor shop in Center City. He had scores of Jackson photos in his shop. As a kid who followed the game, I asked him why he had so many pictures up of Jackson. "Because he's my son," the man said.)

Gillick spent 17 years with the Blue Jays, winning the two consecutive World Series in his final two years and taking the team to the league championship three other times.

After 45 years in baseball, he has already been inducted into Canada's Sport Hall of Fame and is likely a shoe-in for American baseball's Hall of Fame in Cooperstown.

But one of the best moves Gillick made when he joined the Phillies organization turned out to be one thing that he didn't do: get rid of Phillies Manager Charlie Manuel.

Manuel was a good ole' boy who grew up in Virginia. He moved as slow as his hillbilly drawl and carried a barrel belly that hung over his belt.

But the 51st manager of the Phillies knew the right thing about baseball: how to win.

One of 11 children, Manuel played for a few seasons with The Minnesota Twins and New York Yankees, mostly as a pinch-hitter after being drafted right out of high school.

His baseball career didn't take off, though, until he traveled to the most unlikeliest of places for a Pentecostal preacher's son: Japan. He was popular for his home run hitting ability and hustle, dubbed "Aka-Oni," the red devil.

In 1977 alone, he hit .316 with 42 home runs and knocked in close to 100 runners. The following year he did pretty much the same thing, taking his team to their first pennant and championship series. In 1980, the man who was called the Mickey Mantle of Japan set the record for the most home runs by an American with 48. One talent that would serve him well down the line was Manuel's textbook ability to hit.

Manuel returned home and became a minor league manager for 10 years, winning two championships with the Cleveland Indians' farm teams. He was named manager of the year three times.

He returned to the major leagues as a hitting coach for the Indians, who led the American League in runs three times. They set a franchise record in 1999 with 1,009 runs becoming the first team to score 1,000 since 1950.

He eventually became the manager and led the team to the playoffs, winning 91 games. But he was fired in 2002 over a contract dispute while his team had won only 39 games to 48 losses.

Manuel followed the fiery Bowa as the Phillies manager and couldn't have had a more opposite demeanor. The team went from 60 mph to driving the speed limit as Manuel brought a calmness to the locker room and a keen ability to show others how to hit.

Some sports commentators in Philadelphia thought Manuel was too laid back for the players. The numbers, however, didn't jibe. In this season alone, his team scored 799 runs and hit a league-leading 214 home runs on their way to winning 92 games.

September was the make or break month for the 2008 Phillies and they rose to the occasion.

Moyer won eight of his final nine games and the Phillies won 13 of their last 16, putting the Mets in their rear view mirror. In sweet justice, the Mets crashed again in September and were eliminated from the playoffs on the final day of the season for the second consecutive year.

Victorino, nicknamed "The Flyin' Hawaiian" for his speed and native state, had a breakout year, hitting .293 with 14 home runs and 36 stolen bases.

Like a train rolling down hill, Howard's home run production rose as the season wore on. He finished as the league leader with 48 home runs and a contender for his second Most Valuable Player award.

Hamels finished 14 and 10 and Myers won seven of his last nine games since coming up from the minors. But the biggest pitching performance for the season came from Moyer, who finished the year 16-7.

Once again the battle with the Mets went down to the wire when the Phillies clinched the division title just two days before the end of the season. But no matter how they got there, the fightin' Phils were going to the playoffs for the second year in a row.

Chapter 18
October Road

One thing that Hamels didn't have going into the postseason in 2007 was playoff experience.

The 23-year-old was rattled, losing the first game to the Colorado Rockies. Gaining another year of pitching in the big leagues buoyed Hamels' confidence. He was aided immensely by the man who became his mentor, Moyer.

Moyer taught Hamels everything from mental preparation for games to dealing with the media, a special talent in a city with a press considered across the nation to be piranhas. He also taught Hamels how to throw a better change up, the pitch that kept Moyer baffling hitters for decades.

The young Phillies team marched into their first game against the Milwaukee Brewers intent on not being swept as it had by the Rockies the year before.

Hamels provided the foundation in Game 1, pitching eight shutout innings, including carrying a no-hitter into the fifth inning and giving up only two hits for the game. Hamels left with the team winning 3-0.

But Lidge resurrected the ghost of Mitch Williams when he came in to relieve Hamels and drove the 46,000 worried fans to their feet stiff with tension. He allowed one run and put runners on second and third with two outs in the ninth, the winning run at the plate.

But Lidge threw a 93 mph fastball through the swing of the Brewers final batter to preserve the win and keep his save streak, now at 42, alive and giving the Phils their first playoff win since 1993.

"I should buy everyone some Pepto, ease the heartburn a little," Lidge told reporters after the game.

With the first game of the five-game series at hand, the Phillies had to walk into the second match facing the Brewers' pitching monster, C.C. Sabathia. The 6-foot-7, 290-pound Sabathia pretty much pitched the Brewers into the playoffs by throwing on three days rest when pitchers usually pitch every fifth day. Sabathia had won 11 of his last 13 games.

Myers paced the mound for the Phillies and picked up where Hamels left off, throwing seven innings and allowing only two runs and two hits. The Phillies shelled Sabathia, who was taken out after the fourth inning and a grand slam by Shane Victorino.

The at-bat of the game and maybe the series, though, came from Myers himself. The pitcher took 19 pitches fouling them off as the crowd went wild at Myers toughness and eventual walk. The Phillies won the game, 5-2.

The Brewers weren't going to go down easy and bounced back with a 4-1 win in the third game. The tough part about the loss was that it came at the hands of Moyer.

He walked two batters and threw a wild pitch in the first inning. A single up the middle brought two runners home and that was all the Brewers needed for the day, knocking Moyer out of the game in the fourth inning.

If Moyer was going to fall apart, this was the worst time. But you couldn't help but feel sorry for him with the way he pitched throughout the season and for what a good guy he was.

Moyer wasn't all to blame. The middle of the Phillies batting order—Utley, Howard and slugger Pat Burrell—only had four hits for the 28 times they batted in the first three games. That the Phillies still had the series lead was fortunate with the jelly bats. The team had only scored in three innings in the 25 played to that point.

"We're supposed to hit and when we don't, yeah, I'm concerned about it," Manuel told reporters. "But I don't know what you can do right now."

The Brewers pitcher was David Bush, who grew up in

94

suburban Philadelphia rooting for the Phillies. Bush was unkind to his childhood team pitching five and a third innings and giving up only one run. And the Brewers bats came to life getting 11 hits causing us Phillies fans pause. If the Brewers win one more game, it's tied 2-2 with the fifth game a toss-up.

The Phillies weren't about to let that happen. They won the fourth game by a decisive 6-2 margin. Rollins started off the game with a home run and Burrell hit two.

The pitching, the part of the team most fans worried about at the start of the season, continued to be solid thanks to another Gillick recruit, Blanton. Blanton, who had won all of the five games he had pitched for the Phillies since coming to the team, threw seven innings, striking out seven and giving up one run. Phillies starting pitchers had only given up five runs in the 25 innings they pitched.

The sleepy Philadelphia bats were waking up and sent the Phillies into the first league championship game in 15 years.

The team celebrated their win with popping corks and champagne baths in the clubhouse. Rollins even bought a pair of swimming goggles in preparation.

But much like the great teams of the 70s, the Phillies path to the pennant would have to go through the sizzling Los Angeles Dodgers.

The Dodgers were a league surprise thanks to one man: Joe Torre. The prostate cancer survivor coached the New York Yankees to 12 consecutive playoff appearances and won four World Series in his first five years. But he was pushed out of the organization by owner George Steinbrenner for not winning more championships.

Torre actually quit the team after Steinbrenner insulted him by offering the base salary for a manager. Torre saw the handwriting on the wall and walked.

The Dodgers also had their own monster in outfielder Manny Ramirez. Not only could Ramirez consistently launch towering shots for home runs but he was considered one, if not the best, hitters in baseball.

The Phillies marched on, trying to become the first

Philadelphia sports team to win a championship in a quarter of a century. The team's Citizens Bank Park held 46,000 for the first game with the Dodgers and the waving white towels began. The twirling cloth made it look like a snowstorm in the stands.

Hamels again took the mound and again was masterful, pitching seven strong innings. Burrell continued crushing the ball hitting a home run in the sixth inning, along with a two-run homer by Utley to lead the team to a 3-2 victory in the best-of-seven series.

One of the key at bats came in the eighth inning when Ramirez came up. The man who hit .500 in the sweep of the Chicago Cubs to get to the National League championship had already hit a double off the wall. That was just shy of the yellow home run marker at the top of the fence.

Manuel made a trip to the mound to talk to relief pitcher Ryan Madson. Manuel had coached Ramirez when they were with the Indians and instructed Madson on how to pitch to the slugger, who lined the ball softly to third.

Lidge pitched in the ninth shutting down the Dodgers 1-2-3, lights out.

Myers pitched game two and once again, his batting was the surprise. He had three hits—half the total for the previous three seasons—and drove in three runs.

Unlike previous playoff games where the Phils won with homers, the team this time rocked the Dodgers starter, Chad Billingsley, for eight runs and eight hits in less than three innings to take the game 8-5.

But the Phillies clubhouse was anything but exuberant. Manuel was told that his 87-year-old mother, who often dished out team advice, passed away. It was the same day that Shane Victorino learned of his grandmother dying in Hawaii.

The game was also marred by Myers throwing at Ramirez in the first inning. With his dreadlocks tucked under his helmet and his massive arms gripping the bat, Ramirez stood stiff and stared at Myers after the pitch. Ramirez answered with his bat, knocking out a home run that drove in three runs in the game to cut the Phillies lead with a ball that thumped into the stadium's left field flower beds.

I thought throwing at Ramirez could've been a grave error. You didn't want to wake up the Dodgers, the proverbial sleeping dog.

The teams headed back to Los Angeles for the third game and Manuel decided to remain coaching, delaying his mother's funeral. The tensions between the two teams continued when Dodgers pitcher, Hiroki Kuroda, threw a 94-mile-per-hour fastball at Victorino's head, resulting in a bench clearing melee.

Victorino motioned to Kuroda that he didn't mind being thrown at but that he didn't appreciate the head hunting.

Moyer got trounced again, this time for six runs in less than two innings as the Dodgers jumped back into the series with a 7-2 win. It was once again heartbreaking to see Moyer struggling.

Gillick's guys continued to be in the right place at the right time. Matt Stairs, the 40-year-old pinch hitter who had spent 20 years in the league playing for 11 teams, broke a 5-5 tie with a two run homer into right field. The shot evoked memories of Dodger Josh Gibson's famous pinch hit homer in the 1988 World Series. It was Stairs' third pinch home run for the Phillies since being acquired August 30.

Victorino also hit a two-run home run and Lidge shut down the last Dodger batters as the Phillies were now one game away from winning the sixth pennant in their history. And Lidge had nothing but praise for Victorino, another Gillick pickup.

"Victorino's one of those guys who kind of goes under the radar," Lidge told reporters. "But he has home run power from both sides of the plate, incredible speed, a great arm, great defense. He's really a complete player. He's as good as it gets."

The Phillies rode into Game 5 with confidence now that Hamels was going to get his second chance to pitch in the series. And he didn't disappoint. Hamels quieted the Dodgers 5-1 as the Phillies reached the World Series for the first time in 15 years. The 24-year-old star picked up the series Most Valuable Player trophy.

Hamels may not have known the significance of the win. He hadn't been born when the last Philadelphia sports team won its championship a quarter century ago in 1983, the Philadelphia 76ers.

Rollins, who only had two hits in 17 chances during the series, kicked the game off once again with a home run.

Like the heralded teams of the 1970s, the Phillies' minor league squads produced the core of the National League champions. Six players in the clinching game lineup, including Rollins, came from the Phillies farm system, ensuring that the young team will continue as contenders.

Manuel stood in the dugout and watched his team celebrate on the field, the sixth time that the Phillies would be going to the 104-year-old World Series.

Manuel was preparing to fly home to bury his mother. In the clubhouse, he accepted the trophy and thought of his number one fan.

He said: "I guarantee you my mom is watching now."

Chapter 19
Phinally

The Phillies were up against the Tampa Bay Rays in the World Series. The Rays were trying to be this first team ever in baseball to go from last place to first place in a year.

They had good strong, young pitchers. And they had a middle of the batting order that was bruising. And much like the Phillies, they had momentum coming off winning a brutal, yet thrilling, seven-game series with the Boston Red Sox, considered the best team in baseball.

Baseball fans I knew without a team in the series considered the match a toss-up, with many wanting the Rays to win because they had never won the championship before.

If they were going to win the first game at home in St. Petersburg they would have to go through Hamels. Hamels faced another 24-year-old ace in Scott Kazmir. Yet again, Hamels was unbeatable, allowing only five hits in seven superb innings in a 3-2 win to take Game 1 of the seven game series.

The win was lucky because the Phillies went 0 for 13 in failing to bring home runners in scoring position, tying a World Series record. A two-run home run by Utley gave the Phils the lead in the first inning that silenced the Rays fans and their tradition of shaking cow bells.

"I can't think of any other way to quiet them down," Manuel told reporters after the game. "If you want to take the wind out of the sails and you shut the cowbells up and get some home runs, that will do it."

Victorino scored the third run on a ground out and that was

all the Phillies needed.

The Phils lost game two to the Rays 4-2 and again were unable to drive players home in scoring position. Their leadoff man, Rollins, was hitless in 10 chances so far. And Howard, the league's best home run hitter, was silenced. For the series, the Phillies only drove one runner home in 28 chances with runners who had reached second base or beyond.

The Rays picked apart the Phillies with seven singles against Myers, who had a relatively strong seven-inning outing. The Phillies were lucky to be tied in the series going back to Philadelphia.

At home, the series lead was on the line for the team's most struggling pitcher, Moyer. I didn't have a good feeling about it. Though I appreciated Moyer, I wondered whether Manuel should have pitched him in such a critical game after his first two rough playoff outings. But I was impressed by Manuel's loyalty and his standing by the old saying: stick with the dogs that brung you.

Moyer proved me wrong. He gave the team six stellar innings with a determination that earned him his 645th career win and first World Series notch. And because it came a few weeks shy of his 46th birthday, Moyer became the second oldest player in World Series history, beat out solely by Jack Quinn of the 1929 Philadelphia Athletics.

Moyer got big bat help from home runs by Utley, Howard and catcher, Carlos Ruiz. The game was delayed 72 minutes because of rain and ended at 1:47 a.m. Ruiz hit a soft ground ball in the ninth inning that only traveled about 40 feet up the third base line but scored Eric Bruntlett for the 5-4 win and a 2-1 series lead.

The young Rays pitchers were having the same problem the Phillies had the year before in the playoffs, getting nervous and rattled on the mound because of no prior World Series experience.

The fourth game of the World Series was the breakout game that the Phillies, their fans and baseball analysts had been waiting for since the playoffs started. The Phils hit four home runs and won by the football score of 10-2.

Howard homered twice and knocked in five runs, giving him three home runs in his last six trips to the plate. He was only the eighth person in World Series history to hit two homers in a single game and collect five runs batted in.

Blanton pitched seven innings with seven strikeouts and even he slugged a home run, the first pitcher to do so in the last 33 World Series. Jason Werth added another homer in offensive onslaught.

The display of raw power delivered the Phillies in a series where they were only 6 for 47 in bringing home runners who had at least reached second base. No matter how they did it, the Phillies had now won 23 of their last 29 games proving once again that the team with the momentum going into the series was likely to prevail.

While the Phillies got hot, the embers for the key Rays hitters were dying. Carlos Pena and Evan Longoria were hitless in 29 attempts in the series.

The Phillies had a chance to clinch their first World Series in almost three decades in Game 5, where they had their best weapon, Hamels, on the mound.

Game 5 of the 2008 World Series between the Phillies and Rays was arguably the most bizarre championship game in the history of baseball.

The Phillies were 10 outs from clinching the title in a driving rain that turned the infield into a brown swamp. That made it the first World Series game ever to be suspended.

The umpires held off on interrupting the game until a Rays player splashed dangerously into second base, which looked like an island surrounded by water. The Phillies were winning 2-0 at the end of the fifth inning.

In a regular season game, the umpires would have likely ended the contest after the required five innings. But baseball Commissioner Bud Selig vowed that the Phillies would not win the series on a rain-shortened game.

"I would not have allowed a World Series to end this way," Selig told reporters. "We'll stay here until we have to celebrate Thanksgiving."

The Rays scored two runs in the top of the sixth inning and the game was suspended with the score 2-2. What added to the bizarreness of the game was that it was canceled the following night because of the cold weather and another threat of rain.

So on Wednesday a game that started two days earlier was resumed in the bottom of the sixth inning with the Phillies up at bat. One downside was that the Phils had to play the remainder of the game without Hamels, who had already pitched six innings two days earlier.

The Phillies took a 3-2 leads thanks to a double by another unsung player, Geoff Jenkins. The Rays came right back on a homer by one of their fan favorites, Rocco Baldelli, who tied the game in the seventh inning.

The Rays almost took the lead but were snagged when Utley threw out a runner in a tense play at the plate. Burrell came up for the Phillies, slumping with no hits in 13 World Series tries.

Burrell clubbed a double to center field and came home on a single by third baseman Pedro Feliz. The bullpen took over from there and the ball ended up in the hands of Lidge. Since joining the Phillies he was an astonishing 47 for 47 in saves, never losing a game when he came to in to pitch when the Phillies were winning.

I feared that with each consecutive save, the odds that Lidge could lose a game grew greater.

But much like Tug McGraw had done 28 years earlier, Lidge delivered the winning strike. With two outs in the ninth, he threw a slider that crumpled under Eric Hinske's bat for strike three and the second championship in the team's 125 years.

The players rushed the mound to pile on the kneeling Lidge and the raucous celebration began. Howard ran from first base and toppled the pile like a linebacker hitting a runner.

The drought was over. Philadelphia had gone 25 years without any of their major sports teams—baseball, football, basketball and hockey—winning a championship, the longest span in American sports history.

That meant the loyalty, passion and patience of prideful Philadelphia fans had been tested through a total of 100 seasons.

I watched the final pitch on television alone in a hotel room in Baton Rouge, where I was covering elections. As soon as the game ended, I called Philadelphia to the Post house, somehow trying to join the celebration long distance, the next best thing to being there and all that.

Friends were popping champagne corks as fans spilled out into the streets, driving around beeping their horns as if it were New Years Eve, dancing in the streets.

Within what seemed to be seconds after the final pitch, my cell phone rang and I flipped it open. It was Chris O'Keefe in Florida.

"HOW ABOUT 'DEM PHILLIES?!?!?!" he shouted.

Yes my friend. How about them Phillies?

Suggested Further Reading

You Can't Lose Them All, Frank Fitzpatrick, (2001)

Beards, Bellies and Biceps, Robert Gordon and Tom Burgoyne, (2006)

Occasional Glory, David V. Jordan, (2002)

The Phillies Encyclopedia, Rich Westcott and Frank Bilovsky, (2004)

Phillies Essential, Rich Westcott, (2006)

Gerard Shields covered Baltimore city government for three years at The Baltimore Sun. Prior to that, he worked as a government reporter at the Scripps Howard News Service in Washington, D.C., The Allentown Morning Call, The Orlando Sentinel and the Gloucester County Times in New Jersey. He currently serves as the Washington correspondent for The Baton Rouge Advocate.

4544654

Made in the USA
Charleston, SC
08 February 2010